OTHER BOOKS BY MARY MORGAN BROWN

Love Is the Remedy: Poems for a Mending Heart

SEEK, WAIT, TRUST

Poems for Navigating the Spiritual Journey

MARY MORGAN BROWN

Prayers by Rev. Dr. Greggory L. Brown
FOREWORD by Rev. Dr. James A. Forbes, Jr.

Copyright © 2022 Mary Morgan Brown.

All rights reserved. No part of this book may be used or reproduced by any means, graphic, electronic, or mechanical, including photocopying, recording, taping or by any information storage retrieval system without the written permission of the author except in the case of brief quotations embodied in critical articles and reviews.

WestBow Press books may be ordered through booksellers or by contacting:

WestBow Press
A Division of Thomas Nelson & Zondervan
1663 Liberty Drive
Bloomington, IN 47403
www.westbowpress.com
844-714-3454

Because of the dynamic nature of the Internet, any web addresses or links contained in this book may have changed since publication and may no longer be valid. The views expressed in this work are solely those of the author and do not necessarily reflect the views of the publisher, and the publisher hereby disclaims any responsibility for them.

All photographs, including the cover image, were shot by Jeffrey T. Hladik, deceased son of Mary Morgan Brown.

Unless otherwise noted, scripture taken from the Holy Bible, NEW INTERNATIONAL VERSION®, NIV® Copyright © 1973, 1978, 1984, 2011 by Biblica, Inc.® Used by permission. All rights reserved worldwide.

Scripture quotations marked (CEV) are from the Contemporary English Version Copyright © 1991, 1992, 1995 by American Bible Society. Used by Permission.

Scripture marked (Darby) taken from the Darby Bible.

ISBN: 978-1-6642-7573-7 (sc)
ISBN: 978-1-6642-7575-1 (hc)
ISBN: 978-1-6642-7574-4 (e)

Library of Congress Control Number: 2022915311

Print information available on the last page.

WestBow Press rev. date: 11/29/2022

♥ ♥ ♥ ♥

To our parents, Betty & Harold Brown and Dorothy & Ray Morgan, we offer a debt of gratitude for nurturing our spirituality from the first breath we each took. You helped us know, at the core of our beings, that we are beloved children of God. As you lived out the values you taught us, you always modeled your complete trust in God. We thank God for the firm foundation of faith you laid for us and pray we daily pass that on to family, friends, parishioners, and strangers alike. When our time on earth has ended, may we all gather together in heaven as the family of God, saved by grace.

*Seek willingly and actively…gladly and happily,
without foolish sadness and empty sorrow…
wait upon him steadfastly, not grumbling and striving against him…
trust him completely with certainty of hope.
For it is his will that we know he will come suddenly and joyfully to all who love him.*
Julian of Norwich (1342-1416)

CONTENTS

Foreword xi
Preface xv
Acknowledgements xvii

Chapter 1: Seek Actively 1
    A Seeking Prayer 44
Chapter 2: Wait Steadfastly 47
    A Waiting Prayer 102
Chapter 3: Trust Completely 105
    A Trusting Prayer 186

Endnotes 189
Bibliography 191
Index of Poems 193
Index of Biblical References 195
List of Poems by Chapter 197
About the Authors 201

FOREWORD

I knew Greggory Brown as a student at Union Theological Seminary where we became personal friends. But I did not know Mary, his wife, until I had the privilege of reading her collection of poems. They gave me an intimate and close up look at the pilgrimage of a true and trusting servant of the most high God. I discovered she was a faithful follower of Jesus, the Christ.

Her husband was the pastor of the church and the preacher of the congregation and the community. Mary seemed to feel a calling to share in words of poetry what it had been like to take a daily walk listening for the voice of God and meditating on the deep meaning of biblical wisdom and exhortation. As she encountered conflicts, confusion, and crises on the pathway of life, her conversations with God became counseling sessions with the Spirit. Her poems capture time-tested truths by which one could wrestle with the temptations of the evil one. Over many years of agonizing, soul-searching reflection on *seeking*, *waiting*, and *trusting*, her character was forged and solidified into strong Christian maturity. From her treasure trove of spiritual guidance, she was able to offer much needed advice to those who sought her perceptive wisdom or parental encouragement.

During their health struggles and traumas related to sickness and death of loved ones, Gregg and Mary modeled the partnership between brothers and sisters of faith. Therefore, Mary asked Gregg to offer some of his prayers to enrich her collection of poems. It is her hope that just as she found God to be a very present help in times of trouble, those who seek God's strength through these pages will hear a word of hope and feel the comforting touch of the Almighty God.

When I was asked to consider writing the Foreword for Mary Morgan Brown's collection of poems, I wondered what kind of poetry to expect. Would it be like Henry Wadsworth Longfellow's *The Builders?*

> *All are architects of Fate,* *Nothing useless is, or low;*
> *Working in these walls of Time;* *Each thing in its place is best;*
> *Some with massive deeds and great,* *And what seems but idle show*
> *Some with ornaments of rhyme.* *Strengthens and supports the rest.**

---

* William Wadsworth Longfellow, *The Seaside and the Fireside* (Boston: Ticknor, Reed, and Fields, 1850), 55.

Or would it be like Maya Angelou's *Phenomenal Woman*?

> *Pretty women wonder where my secret lies.*
> *I'm not cute or built to suit a fashion model's size*
> *But when I start to tell them,*
> *They think I'm telling lies.*
> *I say,*
> *It's in the reach of my arms,*
> *The span of my hips,*
> *The stride of my step,*
> *The curl of my lips.*
> *I'm a woman*
> *Phenomenally.*
> *Phenomenal woman,*
> *That's me.**

Or would it be more like e.e. cummings's *poem number 65*?

> *i thank You God for most this amazing*
> *day: for the leaping greenly spirits of trees*
> *and a blue true dream of sky; and for everything*
> *which is natural which is infinite which is yes*
>
> *(i who have died am alive again today,*
> *and this is the sun's birthday; this is the birth*
> *day of life and love and wings: and of the gay*
> *great happening illimitably earth)*
>
> *how should tasting touching hearing seeing*
> *breathing any—lifted from the no*
> *of all nothing—human merely being*
> *doubt unimaginable You?*
>
> *(now the ears of my ears awake and*
> *now the eyes of my eyes are opened)***

---

* Maya Angelou, *Four Poems Celebrating Women* (New York: Oxford University Press, 1950), 65.

** e.e. cummings, *Xaipe: seventy-one poems* (New York: Oxford University Press, 1950), 65.

Mary's poems are not like anybody else's. They are not even like each other.

Mary once faced a life and death struggle that was on the verge of murderous consequences. She called out to the Lord for steps to take and words to say. God responded to her cry with the wisdom that saved her life. It is Mary's hope that from these pages, someone will find deliverance in the varied styles and forms that speak life in the face of death.

These poems are not just literary offerings, but also testimonies of what God can do and will do. In many of these poems, scripture verses have morphed into direct advice not so much to be quoted, but actions to be taken.

Listen not so much for rhymes or meter, literal or symbolic intent. Listen with your heart to hear the voice of God. God has heard the interrogatives, intercessions, petitions, and gratitude of your soul and has lovingly placed an answer in your spirit. The divine disclosures may have come in a series of words, several lines, multiple paragraphs, or a number of pages. If you do not discern the meaning on your first reading, read again and again. When you are finally ready, say "Speak Lord, your servant child is ready to hear!"

Thank you, Mary.

Thank you, Greggory.

Thank you, God.

Rev. Dr. James A. Forbes, Jr.
Raleigh, August 2022

PREFACE

This book was born of a Julian of Norwich quote that moved me to tears. *Seek willingly and actively… gladly and happily, without foolish sadness and empty sorrow…wait upon him steadfastly for love, not grumbling and striving against him…trust him completely with certainty of faith. For it is his will that we know he will come suddenly and joyfully to all who love him.*[1] This 14th century nun who lived an obscure life still reaches across 700 years of history to touch the lives of modern seekers in the 21st century.

My husband Gregg and I hope my poems and his prayers will likewise touch your heart. They have been inspired by ancient scriptures that speak of *seeking* God, *waiting* for the knowledge of and the playing out of his will for us, and *trusting* him in all things.

One of the great spiritual writers of the 20th Century, Rev. Dr. Howard Thurman, has influenced the lives of millions as a preacher, professor, philosopher, mentor to Dr. Martin Luther King, Jr., and enlightened mystic. As a young man, Gregg was asked by Bishop T. Garrott Benjamin to drive Dr. Thurman back to the hotel after the dedication of the Thurman Library at Light of the World Christian Church in Indianapolis. As Gregg apologized for the poor condition of his 1963 Chevy Nova, Dr. Thurman said, "Does it have enough gas? Does the engine start? Does it go forward and backwards?" After Gregg nodded affirmatively to each question, Dr. Thurman chuckled, "Well, then, young man, I'm grateful for the ride!" Pragmatic wisdom. His profound insight has moved both of us on many occasions; his words on "seeking God" are no exception:

> *Again and again I am conscious that I am seeking God. There is ever present in me a searching longing for some ultimate resting place for my spirit — some final haven of refuge from storms and upheavals of life. I seek ever the kind of peace that can pervade my total life, finding its quiet way into all the hidden crevices of my being and covering me completely with a vast tranquility. This I seek not because I am a coward, not because I am afraid of life or of living, but because the urge seems to steady me to the very core. With sustained excitement, I recall what, in my own urgency, I had forgotten: God is seeking me. Blessed remembrance! God is seeking*

> me. Wonderful assurance. God is seeking me. This is the meaning of my longing, this is the warp of my desiring, this is my point. The searching that keeps the sand hot under my feet is but my response to His seeking. Therefore, this moment, I will be still, I will quiet my reaching out, I will abide; for to know really that God is seeking me; to be aware of that now is to be found of Him. Then, as if by miracle, He becomes the answer to my need. It sufficeth now and forever that I am found of Him.[2]

God has answered our *needs* so many times in the ten years it took to write this book. We each faced health setbacks and endured emotional trauma, including the passing of three of our four beloved parents and the unexpected death of our wonderful son/stepson, Jeff, whose photography graces this book. God's presence became a *haven of refuge*. It is our hope that our poems and prayers guide you along your own personal journey of faith as you strive to **seek, wait** for, and **trust** the grace-filled Lord we serve.

Mary Morgan Brown
Oakland, September 2021

ACKNOWLEDGEMENTS

I owe many thanks to my family, friends, and colleagues who lifted my spirits, encouraged my perseverance, read numerous drafts, gave editorial assistance, and loved me through the writing process that lasted more than a decade.

An enormous heartfelt thank you goes to my husband, the Reverend Dr. Greggory L. Brown, who put up with endless days of poetic reclusiveness, clouded attentiveness, missed meals, and middle of the night inspirations. Despite all that neglect, Gregg still lovingly agreed to add his charismatic voice and deep devotion to God to this book (see *A Seeking Prayer*, pp. 44-45; *A Waiting Prayer*, pp. 102-103; *A Trusting Prayer*, pp. 186-187). Each of his pastoral prayers were taped and transcribed from live worship services at Miracles of Faith Community Church, ELCA, in Oakland, California, where he is Senior Pastor.

A debt of gratitude goes to the Reverend Dr. James A. Forbes, Jr., Senior Pastor Emeritus of Riverside Church in Manhattan, founder of the Healing the Nations Foundation, and my husband's beloved Professor of Preaching at Union Theological Seminary in New York City. Their friendship has spanned more than three decades. I have been blessed to meet Dr. Forbes and his lovely wife Bettye and to hear him preach on several occasions. It is a great honor to have his touching Foreword add scholarly credibility to our book. Dr. Forbes is one of the "12 Most Effective Preachers" in the English-speaking world (*Newsweek*, 1996), the articulate author of *Whose Gospel? A Concise Guide to Progressive Protestantism* (The New Press, 2010), a poet himself, and a true champion of racial justice, women's equity, and progressive social change.

Special appreciation goes to those mentioned here and many others too numerous to name. My nervous angst over writing slumps and the elusive publishing process was often perceptively neutralized by my dear friend, Robin Fletcher. She, along with Kyle Chermak, Rev. Fred Williams, and Rev. Carol Been, proofread and validated my ever-evolving manuscript. The staff at WestBow Press, in particular Bob DeGroff, were patient and helpful. I also valued the sweet encouragement that I received over the years from the WELCA group at MFCC. You always made me feel heard. Our friend and Gregg's publicist, Jackie Wright, made much welcomed revisions to the About the Authors page.

Thank you all from the bottom of my heart. Such unconditional love ultimately culminated in the publication of *Seek, Wait, Trust: Poems for Navigating the Spiritual Journey*.

My greatest indebtedness, however, goes to God, my Father; Jesus, his Son, my Lord and Savior; and the Holy Spirit, my counselor and guide. I apologetically acknowledge that not everyone is comfortable with male pronouns for God. Please note, as a child of the late 50s and early 60s, I have always experienced the Triune God as masculine, but I am deeply moved by the feminine nature of divinity as well. I want you, dear reader, to feel free to make the necessary gender adjustments to support your own spiritual solace.

Finally, it brings me great joy to include some extraordinary photographs, especially the stunning cover image, taken by my eldest son, Jeffrey T. Hladik. They were discovered in Jeff's Nikon camera shortly after his sudden death in 2019. I have posthumous appreciation for his artistic talent that went unnoticed while my son was alive. May his photographs, my husband's prayers, and my poems tap into a part of your soul that is longing to draw closer to God, craving to feel the Spirit's comfort, and/or yearning to follow Jesus along the journey of faith.

CHAPTER 1:
SEEK ACTIVELY

Seeking Serenity

O God, you are my God, earnestly I seek you. – Psalm 63:1a

Empty Sorrow

I'm struggling
To know
Why
My prayers are so shallow.
I still believe
In you, Lord.
I'm the shaky one,
Not you.
I know how steady
And strong you are.
My spiritual walk
Seems shaky, too,
Like an inept actor
Clumsily wandering
Onstage
To apply for a leading role.

Why can't I recapture
The rapture
I used to feel?
Life's latest staggering blows
Seem to have overshadowed
My normally serene spirit.
The still small voice
Longs to stop
This "foolish sadness".
Help me find solace
In your supportive arms.
Remove this "empty sorrow"
As I "willingly
And actively…
Gladly and happily"[3]
Seek you.

Seek, Wait, Trust

*But if from there you seek the Lord your God,
you will find him if you look with all your heart and with all your Soul.* – Deuteronomy 4:29

In the Midst of the Mess

I remember searching
for a poem I had written years ago.
I thought
it would make
the perfect ending
to a speech I was writing.

I tore the house apart
looking for it.
Finally,
in futile frustration,
I sat in the middle of the room
and cried.

Tears that had been welling up for years,
about people and circumstances
over which I had had no control,
came flooding out.
I cried hysterically for a long time.
At last, gasping for breath, I pleaded,

"God, I need you to rescue me from this pain,
this anxiety,
this self-pity,
this sense of utter hopelessness.
God, please, please help me.
I need to know you're here."

Suddenly, through the haze of tears,
I spotted a pile of papers and books
under the couch . . .
unnoticeable had I not been brought so low.
As I pulled them out,
I screamed in amazement and joy!

Seek Actively

There buried in the midst of the mess
was my Bible,
lost for months since our move across country!
I cradled it in my arms,
as a mother cradles her precious child,
and sobbed and sobbed and sobbed.

Oh, God,
what a humble, defining moment!
Brought to my knees overcome by emotions,
astutely aware that nothing I ever write
will even remotely compare
to the wisdom found in that Holy Book.

Deeply touched by the Lord's profound presence
and awesome awareness of my deepest needs,
I opened my Bible to words
that would not only end my speech,
and this poem,
but also would begin a new chapter of my life:

But if from there
you seek the Lord your God,
you will find him
if you look
with all your heart
and with all your soul.

Seek, Wait, Trust

First seek the counsel of the Lord. – I Kings 22:5

The Master Chef

The Bible says,
First
seek the counsel of the Lord.
Wise advice fit for a king.
Wisdom to pass on
from generation to generation.

But, what do we do *first?*
We "stew" over our problems.
for hours,
for days,
for weeks.
That's a recipe for disaster.

Our tears become the onions,
health concerns the potatoes.
Heartache is the tomato;
sweat and toil make up the broth.
Losses, rather than tofu,
soak up the tainted flavor.

Money qualms replace the meat,
self-pity the celery.
Anxieties are swapped for
"good for you" vegetables.
Next, we season our stew
with doubt, fear, and anxiety.

Why are we then surprised
that far too often
the ingredients we've thrown into the pot
make a horrendous final product?
Starchy…flavorless…
acidic…unsubstantial.

Why do we continually forget
that God is the master chef?
When he spices things up, it's all good!
He will prepare a dish fit for a king,
if we could just learn
to seek him first.

Seek, Wait, Trust

I revealed myself to those who did not seek me. I was found by those who did not seek me. To a nation that did not call on my name, I said, "Here I am, here I am." – Isaiah 65:1

Here I Am

Like every parent,
I've witnessed my child's misbehavior.
She wants something she shouldn't have,
repeatedly asking, "But why?
Why can't I have it?"
She progresses to whining, sulking,
stamping her little foot,
stubbornly ignoring my attempts to calm her.
Withholding her love,
she hisses, "I hate you! You are so mean!"
A full-fledged temper tantrum erupts,
followed by a forced time-out.

This strong-willed child digs in deeper,
seething with anger over this "injustice".
Her loud "Why not?" becomes a non-spoken "Why me?"
Later, when I return to soothe her wounded ego,
I offer comfort.
"It's okay. Mommy's here. You're not alone."
Stubborn little shoulders quiver with relief
as she relaxes into loving arms.
After many sobs, through trembling lips,
she whispers, "I'm sorry. I didn't mean to…"
"I know, I still love you. You're forgiven.
It's okay. Everything will be all right."

Seek Actively

So, too, our Heavenly Father reveals himself to us
even when we've behaved badly,
even when we're at our most vulnerable,
even before we deserve his attention.
He reaches out with such pure compassion
and gently lets us know,
Here I am. Here I am.
By his grace,
we are forgiven.
"All shall be well"[4]
because God loves us
unconditionally.

Seek, Wait, Trust

> *Seek the Lord while he may be found; call on him while he is near.*
> *Let the wicked forsake his way and the evil man his thoughts.*
> *Let him turn to the Lord, and he will have mercy on him,*
> *and to our God, for he will freely pardon.* – Isaiah 55:6-7

Change Me

Have I become so selfish
that I can't even see
my neighbor's pain –
let alone feel it?
Yet you, Lord,
bear his burden,
while I seek pleasure
rather than truth.

Have I become so secure
that I can't even see
her frozen fear –
let alone feel it?
Yet you, Lord,
calm her fears,
while I seek safety
rather than serenity.

Have I become so full
that I can't even see
his haunting hunger –
let alone feel it?
Yet you, Lord,
feed his body, mind, and soul,
while I seek with greed
rather than with grace.

Have I become so content
that I can't even see
their hopelessness –
let alone feel it?
Yet you, Lord,
grant them the power of the Holy Spirit,
while I seek the ways of the world
rather than the kingdom of God.

Seek Actively

Forgive my self-centeredness,
and calm my fear of involvement.
I seek to be your disciple.
Feed me your bread of life;
let me become your broken body for others.
Radically change me, Lord,
before I cause additional pain
with my apathy.

Humble me at the foot of your cross
and open my insensitive eyes.
I seek to serve others in the light of your love.
Serve me the wine that redeems us all;
let me feel connected to others through you.
Radically change me, Lord,
before my indifference nails another hole
in your outstretched hands.

Seek, Wait, Trust

The Lord is with you when you are with him. If you seek him, he will be found by you, but if you forsake him, he will forsake you. – II Chronicles 15:2

Source of Strength

People throughout history
have cried the same desperate lament,
"Oh, God, where are you?"
Amid the world's death and destruction,
"Where are you?"

Yet, the ancient answer remains the same,
I am with you when you are with me.
If you seek me, I will be found by you,
but if you forsake me,
I will forsake you.

And humble seekers have stepped forward
with the God of creation
as the source of their strength and courage
to change
the course of history.

At this critical moment in time,
despite the world's current disrespect
for one another and for God,
the disillusioned bark out their blame,
"Where is your God?"

But the ancient answer remains the same:
I am with you when you are with me.
If you seek me, I will be found by you,
but if you forsake me,
I will forsake you.

Will God's courageous people
please step forward
with inner strength
to change history?
Creation needs saving.

But seek first his kingdom and his righteousness, and all these things will be given to you as well. – Matthew 6:33

But seek his kingdom, and these things will be given to you as well. – Luke 12:31

Seeking the Kingdom

If we're really seeking God's kingdom,
we'd do more than just talk about justice:
paying back those we owe four-fold,
selling half of what we own
to give away to the poor,
or at least giving away what we don't need.
The peace, the love, the compassion
we nurture here on earth
is what we can expect to receive
in the eternal realm.

If we're really seeking God's righteousness,
we'd be more like Jesus:
communing with the poor and the outcasts,
visiting the sick and the imprisoned,
or looking as close as the person next to us
whose needs we have up to now ignored.
The same way we treat
the least of these
is the way we may be treated
at the final judgment.

The kingdom of God
should be more than our future hope;
it should also be our present reality.
Are we doing God's will
right here,
right now?
The peace, the love, the compassion
we nurture here on earth
is what we might expect to receive
when the heavenly kingdom comes.

Seek, Wait, Trust

Sow for yourself righteousness, reap the fruit of unfailing love, and break up your unplowed ground; for it is time to seek the Lord, until he comes and showers righteousness on you. – Hosea 10:12

It Is Time

Sow for yourself righteousness,
Do good.
Be just.
Avoid being judgmental.

Reap the fruit of unfailing love.
Cherish your family.
Cultivate lifelong friendships.
Appreciate grace.

And break up your unplowed ground.
Make a radical new beginning.
Be repentant.
Become productive for the Lord.

For it is time to seek the Lord until he comes.
Be centered.
Stay faithful.
Trust in his return.

He showers righteousness upon you.
He keeps his promises
And blesses you in mighty ways.
Remain loyal to him.

Beloved, let us love one another; because love is of God, and every one that loves has been begotten of God, and knows God. He that loves not has not known God; for God is love. – I John 4:7-8 (DARBY)

And we know that in all things God works for the good of those who love him, who have been called according to his purpose. – Romans 8:28

"I will send my messenger, who will prepare the way before me. Then suddenly the Lord you are seeking will come to his temple; the messenger of the covenant, whom you desire, will come," says the Lord Almighty. – Malachi 3:1

Don't Doubt God's Love

Don't doubt God's love;
he will keep his covenant.
As the God of history,
he is the gold bullion of our existence.
Prophets and messengers,
as well as ordinary people like you and me,
can attest to his steadfast love.
John the Baptist prepared the way for the promised one
who came to offer forgiveness
and newfound freedom from sin.
The son of righteousness,
like the sun that always rises,
provides a light in the darkness
glowing with God's grace…
Love made manifest.

Don't doubt God's loving presence;
he is as close as a whispered prayer.
Everything is working for good
according to his plans for you because you love the Lord.
Live by faith, not sight.
Let go of your anxieties.
You don't have to understand all things;
great mysteries abound too vast for human understanding.
Just know God's love is real.
He will never leave or abandon you.
Feel his tenderness.
Know he is your guarantee.
He cares for you in ways you cannot fathom.
Even when you feel most unlovable,
let God love you *for God is love.*

Seek, Wait, Trust

He answered, "'Love the Lord your God with all your heart and with all your soul and with all your strength and with all your mind'; and, 'Love your neighbor as yourself.'" – Luke 10:27

Blessed are they who keep his statutes and seek him with all their heart. I seek you with all my heart; do not let me stray from your commands. Seek your servant, for I have not forgotten your commands. – Psalm 119:2, 10, 176b

Finding Our Way Back

God wants us to be with him,
but we have become a society
of lost sheep
wandering off on our own.
Immersed in the world's ways,
we feel susceptible to its danger.
Yet God has not left us alone.
From the very beginning,
he has shown us
how to find
our way back to him.

We must follow his commands:
put him first;
idolize nothing else;
praise his holy name;
find rest in him;
respect our parents;
value life
and relationships;
be trustworthy;
avoid tearing each other down;
and be satisfied with what we have.

Since our independent spirits
continue to lead us astray,
God has sent his son to teach us the way:
love the Lord God
with all our heart and soul and mind
and love our neighbors as ourselves.
When we stray from these life lessons,
Jesus, the great shepherd,
meets us where we are
and brings us back into the fold
if we are still seeking God.

Seek the Lord, all you humble of the land, you who do what he commands. Seek righteousness, seek humility; perhaps you will be sheltered on the day of the Lord's anger. – Zephaniah 2:3

Children of God

On our spiritual journey,
many of us are like children
learning to care for our first pet.
We're clumsy and awkward,
forgetful and inconsistent,
selfish and undependable.

Like the child maturing
into his responsibilities,
seeking a firm relationship with the Lord
makes us more selfless and steadfast,
caring and compassionate,
loving and loyal.

Like the young boy protecting
his prized companion from all danger,
we must provide for those in need,
work for peace and justice,
pursue righteousness
and confront evil.

May we be recognizable
as children of God
by our behavior,
humility
and quest
for the common good.

Seek, Wait, Trust

And you, my son Solomon, acknowledge the God of your father, and serve him with wholehearted devotion and with a willing mind, for the Lord searches every motive behind the thoughts. If you seek him, he will be found by you; but if you forsake him, he will reject you forever. – I Chronicles 28:9-10

Heart, Mind and Soul

Physical well being
Is invaluable.
If we are too sedentary,
We lose years off our lives.
Daily exercise and a healthy lifestyle
Keep our bodies in shape
From the womb to the tomb.

An alert brain
Is priceless.
If we don't use it,
We lose it.
Reading, writing, thinking
Keep our minds alert
From the womb to the tomb.

Spiritual well-being
Is precious.
If we reject God,
We do so to our own self-destruction.
Prayer and meditation
Keep the Lord as close as our own heartbeat
From the womb to the tomb.

You, O God,
Have always promised,
If we seek you with all our heart, mind & soul,
Then you will be found by us.
Your steadfastness and grace
Keep our lives grounded
From the womb to the tomb.

Seek Actively

Evil men do not understand justice, but those who seek the Lord understand it fully. – Proverbs 28:5

The Fine Line

From an early age we are taught:
To listen to our conscience;
To do what is right
In the eyes of the Lord;
And to treat others
As we want to be treated.
A sense of fairness
Draws a fine line between good and evil…
Proverbial wisdom calls it *justice*.

Too soon life experiences
And ever-present
Negative influences
Expose us
To the seductive lure
Of lust, laziness,
Envy, excessiveness,
Arrogance, anger,
And greed.

If we still want to do what is just and good,
God promises to be a light in the darkness
Making visible
Not only the fine line
Between right and wrong,
But also, the unjust lines that separate us.
Those who seek the Lord
Understand justice
Fully.

Seek, Wait, Trust

Love truth and peace. Let us go at once to entreat the Lord and seek the Lord almighty. I myself am going. And many peoples and powerful nations will come to Jerusalem to seek the Lord Almighty.
– Zechariah 8:19b, 21b, 22a

Urgency

Have we lost our urgency
in seeking out the Lord?
Do we really think
we can handle life
on our own?

God asks us to *love truth and peace*.
Truth is justice; peace is love.
Do we really think
we can achieve them
on our own?

Let us go at once.
We need to seek the Lord.
Do we really think
anyone but the creator
can save us now?

I myself am going
to pray and plead
that peace on earth
and in our hearts
will come at last.

Taste and see that the Lord is good; blessed is the man who takes refuge in him…those who seek the Lord lack no good thing. – Psalm 34:8, 10b

I Choose to Believe

I choose to believe because I see you
in the rainbow at the end of a storm,
taking my breath away as it appears,
showing your love in an infinite form.

I choose to believe because I hear you
in the joyful sounds of hymns filled with praise,
lifting my wounded world-weary spirit,
giving renewed hope on my darkest days.

I choose to believe because I smell you
in the fresh spring scent of flowers and trees,
glistening with dew in the morning air,
dancing with delight in the daybreak's breeze.

I choose to believe because I taste you
in communion bread and wine being served,
offering your life as a sacrifice,
becoming the love none truly deserved.

I choose to believe because I feel you
in grateful stories of the newly saved,
sharing how they have radically changed,
taking refuge on the path you have paved.

I choose to believe because you touch me
in the innermost corners of my soul,
sensing your compassion and tenderness,
knowing I was broken but now am whole.

Seek, Wait, Trust

By myself I can do nothing: I judge only as I hear, and my judgment is just, for I seek not to please myself but him who sent me. – John 5:30

The Way

God certainly wants us to obey,
so he sent his Son to show the way.
Everything our Savior would do
required knowledge of God's point of view.
Truly Jesus sought God's will and way,
not earthly pleasures every day.

Each time Jesus faced evil and sin,
he sought his Father through thick or thin.
Even when crucified on the cross
he counted his death as gain not loss.
Such sacrifice brings us face to face
with pain that precedes ultimate grace.

In order to do God's will on earth,
we need a spiritual rebirth.
Then we will seek God in all we do
and notice our blessings in plain view.
We will learn to let go of sorrow
with faith in a better tomorrow.

I love those who love me, and those who seek me find me. – Proverbs 8:17

The Best Way

The best way to find is to seek;
The best way to be loved is to love.
The best way to be forgiven is to forgive;
The best way to receive is to give.

The best way to get a smile is to give one away;
The best way to laugh is to share the laughter with others.
The best way to assemble answers is to question with yearning;
The best way to gain knowledge is to truly love learning.

The best way to solve problems is to seek win-win solutions;
The best way to create community is to warmly welcome the stranger.
The best way to avoid loneliness is to give comfort to a lonely soul;
The best way to feel connected is to be a part of the whole.

The best way to be heard is to listen actively;
The best way to get a hug is to give a hug.
The best way to live life is to live it gratefully;
The best way to obtain justice is to treat others fairly.

The best way to be happy is to spread joy;
The best way to do good is to be good.
The best way to have a friend is to be a friend;
The best way to spend time with God is from day's beginning to end.

Seek, Wait, Trust

> *Who may ascend the hill of the Lord? Who may stand in his holy place?*
> *The one who has clean hands and a pure heart, who does*
> *not trust in an idol or swear by a false god.*
> *They will receive blessing from the Lord and vindication from God their Savior.*
> *Such is the generation of those who seek him, who seek your face, God of Jacob.* – Psalm 24:3-6

Providing an Anchor

How can we blame
some of the younger generation
for their thoughtless apathy,
their inability to feel
and reason,
their cowardly acts of violence?
They demand respect
but can't give it.

No one has taught them
to respect their elders
let alone you, O God.
They do not know of your saving acts of mercy
or how to lean on you as the source
of their inner strength.
Plus, some adults in their lives
don't always deserve their respect.

They do not know how to seek,
let alone
praise you.
No one has taught them
of your wondrous miracles
or that your spirit
dwells in the center
of the human heart...

the center from which springs
emotion,
thought,
motivation,
courageous action,
and love.
The blame does not rest
solely on these children.

Seek Actively

May our ability
to show gratitude
in challenging times,
as well as in moments
of profound joy,
provide an anchor
in the lives of young people
drifting alone.

If we are to save
this generation and the next,
we must live out our faith in our daily lives,
seeking and praising you
in a way that is honest and true.
Help our rejoicing hearts
attract your children
to you, oh Lord.

There are other young people
who are fighting for racial justice.
police reform,
a cleaner environment,
saner gun control,
and an end to senseless violence.
Rather than us saving them,
they may be saving us and the world you gave us.

Anchor us all
to your merciful love
and righteous justice.
Bless us, Lord,
and help us to teach our children
to respect and seek you
for guidance and answers
in all they do.

Seek, Wait, Trust

I sought the Lord, and he answered me; he delivered me from all my fears. – Psalm 34:4

But may all who seek you rejoice and be glad in you; may those who long for your saving help always say, "The Lord is great!" – Psalm 70:4

Glory in his holy name; let the hearts of those who seek the Lord rejoice. Look to the Lord and his strength; seek his face always. – Psalm 105:3-4

Seeking His Guidance

Precious is my quiet time every day.
Prayer and meditation help overcome
Former scars and rejections that left me numb.
I'm now grateful for each day that comes my way.

I spend time with God and place my hope in him.
With a joyful heart, I pledge to do his will.
Faith replaces fear, and when I'm very still,
God's presence feels like a calm, comforting hymn.

As I patiently pray for pure peace of mind,
I try to let go of judgmentalism
For God's light alone is the perfect prism.
My heart longs to be loving, humble and kind.

I must keep in mind God uses each defect,
And everything does happen for a reason.
Surrendering is needed in each season
As my creator continues to perfect.

I might miss the miracles God has in store,
Unless my moral compass faces the Lord
And within me his strength and power are poured.
Seeking his guidance is never a closed door.

"For I know the plans I have for you," declares the Lord, "plans to prosper you and not to harm you, plans to give you hope and a future. Then you will call on me and come and pray to me, and I will listen to you. You will seek me and find me when you seek me with all your heart." – Jeremiah 29:11-13

God Is Still in Charge

I find such comfort in this promise:
*For I know the plans I have for you,"
declares the Lord,
"plans to prosper you
and not to harm you,
plans to give you hope and a future.
Then you will call on me
and come and pray to me,
and I will listen to you.
You will seek me and find me
when you seek me with all your heart."*

When life presses down on me,
not only will God protect me—
he has a plan for me—
a plan to get me through
each painful predicament
to a place where I can thrive.
Unlike the stress of college planning,
the anxiety of wedding planning,
or the dread of succession planning,
it is comforting to know
God is still in charge.

This is the very verse
I come back to most often,
because it is full of hope,
grounds me in faith,
and helps me focus and persevere.
I clearly see
the many spots in my life
where God restored my soul:
times when,
in hindsight,
I was actively seeking him.

Seek, Wait, Trust

So I say to you: Ask and it will be given to you; seek and you will find; knock and the door will be opened to you. For everyone who asks receives; he who seeks finds; and to him who knocks, the door will be opened. – Luke 9:10

Letting Go

Only love moves me toward you,
O Lord.
For open arms,
A sweet spirit of joy,
And a faithful friendship
Are closest to the kind expression
Of compassion
I find in your grace and mercy.

If I, instead,
Let anger stew,
Then I move dangerously
Away from you—
Clenching my teeth and my fists,
Acting in curt, un-Christlike ways,
Harboring a grudge,
Seeking imagined ways of revenge.

Like a child
Picking at an infected scab,
Mean thoughts have a way of festering.
Instead of a smile, others see a scowl;
Instead of a song, a hiss;
Instead of beauty, ugliness;
Instead of hope, dread;
Instead of freedom, fear.

Move me away from all-consuming,
self-righteous anger.
Help me learn to let go
Of people and circumstances
Over which I have no control.
Instead let me seek and find you.
Let me knock and discover you
At the door with welcoming arms.

Ask and it shall be given to you; seek and you will find; knock and the door will be opened to you. For everyone who asks receives; he who seeks finds; and to him who knocks, the door will be opened.
– Matthew 7:7-8

Lessons in Love

Just as a gymnast can't afford to hesitate,
I can't give up on myself
Or my purpose for being.
Lessons in love are the reason we live,
The preliminaries
To deciphering what truly matters,
And the key
To discovering our destiny.

Knocking on the door
Seeking his presence in my life,
I concentrate first
On what it means
To love
And be loved by God
So I can negotiate
This balance beam of life.

To gain equilibrium,
Uniqueness,
Flexibility and grace,
I must learn to also value myself.
Like fine-tuning a floor routine,
I'm actively correcting past mistakes,
Making necessary changes,
Developing my natural talents.

With Olympic determination,
I'll keep striving for a perfect 10!
I'll need God's help,
Christ's example,
And the Holy Spirit's zeal
To eagerly finish the work
I was born to do…
Love others.

Seek, Wait, Trust

> *If my people, who are called by my name, will humble themselves*
> *and pray and seek my face and turn from their wicked ways,*
> *then will I hear from heaven and forgive their sins and will heal their land.* – II Chronicles 7:14

Newfound Clarity

"Father, help us
to honor your name."[*]
You love us
infinitely more than our earthly fathers.
Let the world know us
as cherished children of God.

"Come and set up your kingdom."
Help us to be happy and positive
as we share the good news
of the Gospel.
Let the world know us
as faithful kingdom-builders.

God, our creator,
none of us is your equal.
Humble us as we *seek* to do your will on earth,
born anew through your son Jesus.
Let the world know us
as your new creation.

"Give us each day the food we need."
Nourish us in body and soul,
providing not only our daily bread
but also our spiritual sustenance.
Let the world know us
as your grateful family.

"Forgive our sins as we forgive everyone
who has done wrong to us."
You not only forgive us,
but them as well.
Let the world know us
as people who *turn from their wicked ways*.

---

[*] Words in quotation marks are from the Lord's Prayer in Luke 11:1-4 (CEV); words in italics are from the Bible verse above.

Holy One,
we are connected to you through love,
Hear what tempts us
and "deliver (us) from evil."
Let the world know us
as the redeemed of the Lord.

In you, O Lord, lies true "power".
When we reveal our deepest needs to you,
you change us in mighty ways
and dwell within us as the Holy Spirit.
Let the world know us
as pure light in these dark times.

Everlasting God,
your son taught us to love you,
our neighbors, and even our enemies.
He also promised us life eternal.
Let the world know us
as "forever" blessed.

Seek, Wait, Trust

But without faith it is impossible to please Him, for he who comes to God must believe that He is, and He is a rewarder of those who diligently seek Him. – Hebrews 11:6

Keep Believing in God

Keep believing in God.
He will always love you.
From before birth to after death
and in each present moment,
"God is love."*

Don't worry about pleasing others.
Human adulation
ebbs and flows
like the waves at the seashore.
"God is faithful."**

Pursue God minute to minute with faith,
day by day with hope,
year after year with love,
and your soul will surge with serenity.
"God…is a great and awesome God."***

Although family may not always appreciate you,
and some people may take you for granted
while others may not even notice you,
your crown of glory awaits you in the life to come.
God *is a rewarder of those who diligently seek him.*

---

* I John 4: 8b
** I Corinthians 1:9
*** Deuteronomy 7:21

The Lord reigns forever; he has established his throne for judgment. He will judge the world in righteousness; he will govern the people with justice. The Lord is the refuge of the oppressed, a stronghold in times of trouble. Those who know your name will trust in you, for you, Lord, have never forsaken those who seek you. – Psalm 9:7-10

Seeking Justice

We can't seek justice for all without first seeking God;
yet fewer and fewer follow the spiritual path.
More and more openly profess their agnosticism.
Emboldened atheists have ravaged town after town
in their quest to wipe out religious symbols and creeds…
all in the name of religious freedom.

God is infinitely bigger than those symbolic images and doctrines.
If he truly lived in the hearts and minds and souls of the people,
all would still be well.
But our lack of social conscience,
and our love affair with guns and violence and war,
have desensitized us as individuals and as a nation.

God once was our stronghold in times of trouble.
In America, the great breeding ground of democracy,
we have allowed justice to be compromised.
Our courts are cold, callous, and corrupt,
filling prisons to the brim with the poor and marginalized,
the costs of prisons outdistancing the cost of education.

God will judge the world in righteousness
while our government pardons those with political pull,
balances the budget on the backs of the poor and elderly,
and cages children it labels "illegal" or incorrigible.
If we are truly seeking God,
we must work to right these wrongs.

Biblical warnings against oppressing the widow,
the alien and the poor
remind us that the Lord is *the refuge of the oppressed*.
We, who cry out against injustice, must continue
to oppose repression and treat others fairly,
trusting in God's ultimate justice.

*Glory in his holy name; let the hearts of those who seek the Lord rejoice.
Look to the Lord and his strength; seek his face always.
Remember the wonders he has done, his miracles, and the
judgments he pronounced.* – I Chronicles 16:10-12

Humbled by the Crown of Thorns

Like a caged lion,
he approaches the altar—
guarded, cautious, anxious.
He has arrived early to answer an ad for a carpenter,
but in this sacred sanctuary,
his deeper prayer is to be freed
from a life of poverty, deprivation, despair.

She has taken refuge in this stately, old church
after a friend's last-minute cancellation to a nearby play
left her standing shivering in the rain
without a ticket to the sold-out performance.
Praying for a place of deeper connection,
she is profoundly moved by the warmth of the spirit
inside this cold, damp setting.

Unaware of another's presence,
ostrich-like, she takes a blind leap forward in faith.
Both sets of eyes become fixed on the cross
calling them into relationship with their Lord.
Suddenly, their eyes meet.
His seem smoldering with rage,
masking deeper layers of imagined inadequacies.

Embedded fear and an engrained air of privilege
leave her eyes burdened with guilt, shrouded in loneliness.
Jesus' words from the cross to his mother and beloved disciple
seem to hauntingly echo across the racial barriers
that divide these two strangers:
"Woman behold thy son!"
"Behold your mother!"*

More words are buried deep in each soul:
"Father, forgive them for they know not what they do."**
His need to survive,
to hope again,

---

* John 19:26b-27
** Luke 23:34a

to live a life of dignity
is far removed from her desire to move beyond
her insular suburban upbringing.

In this dark, deserted city church,
the panic in her head silently shouts,
"Don't hurt me; I've come in peace!"
The unvoiced anger in his hisses, "You don't belong here!
I'll get my freedom on my own terms, not yours."
But both remain silent
and kneel to pray, reflecting on…

the pierced side…the nail holes…the sacrificial lamb
asking them to lay down their differences at the foot of His cross.
"Father, into your hands I commit my spirit."[*]
Through her tear-streaked eyes, she suddenly sees the face of Jesus
in this man's serene expression as he, too, walks forward to receive communion.
He hears his Savior's command to love our enemies reverberating.
His ears hear this woman's unspoken pain; his eyes see her fragile suffering.

The young priest whispers Christ's words:
"This is my body, which is for you; do this in remembrance of me."[**]
Each body and spirit broken in need of acceptance and love.
"The new covenant in my blood, which is poured out for you."
replacing
rivers of alienation,
disharmony,
and distrust.

No words are exchanged—
just God's amazing grace.
Humbled by the crown of thorns,
they are sent forth to love others
as they could never have
loved
before.

---

[*] Luke 23:46
[**] I Corinthians 11:24

Seek, Wait, Trust

For the Son of Man came to seek and to save what was lost. – Luke 19:10

Saving What Was Lost

If you've ever
been lost,
you know
the engulfing fear,
the paralyzing panic,
the loneliness
and hopelessness
that overwhelm you.

Jesus comes to seek and save
those who are lost,
including you and me.
He brings calm serenity,
perfect peace,
a sense of belonging
and the hope of salvation
to uphold and uplift.

Resolve to seek
and serve God
with the same passion.
In his presence,
weep for joy
like a lost child
who has been safely
returned home.

And each time
you attract someone new
to the kingdom of God,
sigh with relief
like the grateful parent
of a beloved child
who once was lost
but now is found.

The Lord looks down from heaven on the sons of man to see if there are any who understand, any who seek God. – Psalm 14:2

A Beacon of Hope

Faithful
persistent
earnest
seekers
discover a lantern of knowledge
in the Holy Word
where God's glory
transcends human understanding.

Humble
patient
contemplative
spiritual children of God
discover inner calm,
when the Lord's light
shines in the darkest corners
of their troubled souls.

Even lost
anxious
worldly
non-believers
may discover a beacon of hope
in the light and spirit
emanating from those
who love the Lord.

Seek, Wait, Trust

> *One thing I ask of the Lord, this only do I seek: that I may dwell in the house of the Lord all the days of my life, to gaze on the beauty of the Lord and to seek him in his temple… My heart says of you, "Seek his face!" Your face, Lord, I will seek.* – Psalm 27:4, 8

Can It Be?

Can it be that our God,
shines his light in human hearts?
Making his glory known,
is that where compassion starts?

Each morning draws us near
to the Lord's strong embrace;
he smiles with pure delight
seeing souls seeking his face.

Can it be that our God,
who created earth and heav'n,
whispers to those who hear
to protect his creation?[*]

We know that in the dark,
God said, "Let there be light!"
and with that one command,
he created day and night.

Can it be that our God
wants our ever-flowing praise?
See how he shaped the sky
to surround us all our days.

And with His great wisdom
both water and the land
with all that they contain
were created by his hand.

Can it be that our God,
made the sun to shine its light
to show his constant love
as we turn from wrong to right?

Our glowing hearts are like
the moon and stars above
when our creator God
fills us with the Spirit's love.

---

[*] Middle verses based on the creation story in Genesis 1

Seek Actively

Can it be that our God,
who created fowl and fish
and all the animals
wants us to fulfill his wish?

See how they need our help
stopping their extinction.
We're stewards of their care
and must guard all creation.

Can it be that our God
offers life-sustaining peace?
When we draw close to him,
all our fears we can release.

Kneeling in the Lord's house,
we come to offer praise
and learn what we can do
to pursue him all our days.

Can it be that our God
expects us to save his earth?
Knowing our human flaws,
he gives us recharged rebirth.

Earth knows now is the time!
It does no good to hide.
We must each do our part.
Nature needs us on her side!

Seek, Wait, Trust

God did this so that men would seek him and perhaps reach out for him and find him, though he is not far from each of us. "For in him we live and move and have our being." – Acts 17:27-28a

God Reaches Back

Seeking God, our creator, evidence is everywhere…
in a mother gently embracing her newborn child
or a rainbow breaking through storm clouds,
in the sunrise beaming on a bright new day
and light rays skipping across the surface of a serene lake.

Reaching out for him, God reaches back…
in his compassion to forgive
or his pleasure in creating newness,
in his closeness when we need him most
and his unconditional love.

Finding God is part of his master plan…
a reflection of the Lord's magnetism.
He is as near as the air we breathe.
For in him we live and move
and have our being.

Because of the Lord's great love we are not consumed, for his compassions never fail. They are new every morning; great is your faithfulness. I say to myself, "The Lord is my portion; therefore I will wait for him." The Lord is good to those whose hope is in him, to the one who seeks him; it is good to wait quietly for the salvation of the Lord." – Lamentations 3:22-26

Unconditional Love

I won't pretend this is easy.
Losing my mother is like losing a part of my body and soul.
My mother is utterly irreplaceable.
Gratefully, she lives eternally in my heart.

Her unlimited hugs always allowed me to feel cherished.
Her love was as absolute as the daily sunrise,
as demonstrative as a full harvest moon,
and as limitless as the stars in the sky.

My mother's affection was as free as God's amazing grace.
As a child, I idolized her beauty,
I treasured her soothing songs,
and I laughed at her silly jokes.

My mom was a ray of sunshine,
a melodious mockingbird,
a ready reason to smile,
the first one to call and the last one to fear.

I still feel her presence when I see someone smiling,
or hear a soprano singing "I Believe",
or witness a child being comforted by a mother's unconditional love.
As I *wait quietly* with the Lord, *his compassions never fail.*

Seek, Wait, Trust

May the Lord, who is good, pardon everyone who sets their heart on seeking God. – II Chronicles 30:18c-19a

Seek Actively

Seeking God

Every morning

Every day

Keeps us open to his guidance.

Adoring and praising the Lord

Counting our blessings

Taking time to pray

Inviting *the Lord, who is good,* into our hearts

Viewing salvation as a gift of grace

Enduring pain and disappointment

Living each day in service to others

Yields love that will outlive us.

This is what the Lord says to Israel: "Seek me and live."—Seek the Lord and live—Seek good, not evil that you may live. Then the Lord God Almighty will be with you, just as he says he is. – Amos 5:4, 6a, 14

The Open Door

A crushing blow to the chest,
A stabbing pain,
Shortness of breath,
Light headedness,
A quick prayer,
"Lord, let me live."

The intervention of medical science,
Many skilled hands,
Much combined knowledge,
Multiple tests and procedures,
But only one God, my creator,
Who directs the path
Of my life and my heart.

The doctor said he witnessed
The closed valve open
Before the cardiac catheter touched it.
Even this skeptical man of science
Called it a miracle.
To me, it was more than a miracle;
It was the answer to my spiritual quest.
The Lord answered, *Seek me and live.*

A SEEKING PRAYER

I love you, O God, in the blessed name of Jesus,

I yearn for something only you can give…wrap your arms around me and let me hold my God. I seek a deep and lasting relationship with you. Like David, I know that you are:

- My strength
- My rock
- My fortress
- My deliverer
- My God
- My mountain
- My shield
- My salvation
- My stronghold

You are also my helper. Nothing can break my love and trust in you. Even when I'm weary, bless me, Lord, to continue the work of your church, your ministry, and your mission.

If the Israelites survived 40 years in the wilderness because of your faithfulness, make my back strong to handle anything life throws at me. Rescue me from my enemies, for you are my Lord and my God. Give me the courage to call on you to be my rock as I strive to continue to make a difference in this world. Let me never be ashamed of the Gospel of Jesus Christ.

Lord, your power is in plain view daily in the blue sky, the bright golden sunlight, and the green trees and hills. Help me and the flock I lead to seek our refuge in you, the one true God, our hope and our deliverance. We praise you because you are worthy to be praised and to receive glory and honor.

Gracious are you, O God, that you promised to meet all those who come before you seeking your deliverance from our fears and anxieties. You have made it known to those who love you that you are the rock, you are the hope of all generations.

Father God, you come as the beginning, and you draw us close to the end. In your Holy Word, we see grace anchored in the very knowledge of knowing that where there is Jesus there is liberty, where there's the Holy Spirit there's the gift of freedom. We thank you for your Son Jesus. "He was pierced for our transgressions; he was crushed for our iniquities...and by his wounds we are healed."* "He bore our sins in his body on the cross, so that we might die to sins and live in righteousness."** Oh, precious is the name of Jesus.

We pray today that we might be the rocks of Thy salvation, we might be the hope of Thy grace. Help us to bring about necessary change, to do a new thing in your name. Help us to walk in the godliness of caring and nurturing your children. Bless the torch that's keeping the flames of justice ignited that we might march, vote and act to end discrimination and racial practices that attempt to keep people of color oppressed in these United States of America. Break open the silence that allowed the historical enslavement of human life with a new megaphone of true equity.

May the fruits of the Spirit be in us for these are the prayers of your people. May each of us find strength and direction in your Holy Word and in the example of your Son, our Lord and Savior, Christ Jesus, in whose name I pray. Amen.

The Lord Is My Rock

---

*   Isaiah 53: 5
** I Peter 2:24a

CHAPTER 2:
WAIT STEADFASTLY

Waiting in Awe

I remain confident of this: I will see the goodness of the Lord in the land of the living. Wait for the Lord; be strong and take heart and wait for the Lord. – Psalm 27:13-14

Wait for the Lord

*I will see the goodness of the Lord
in the land of the living.
Wait for the Lord;
be strong and take heart
and wait for the Lord.*

Having had a heart attack
one week ago,
these words resonate.
Thankfully I find myself
still among the living.

In my weakened physical state,
I can do nothing but wait!
This physical setback
is an opportunity to ponder
the path my life has taken.

Like warm breath on a bathroom mirror,
my faint pulse
gives credence to this spiritual blessing.
Pulsing with new life,
let me continue to see God in all things.

Asked to *take heart*,
after my fragile heart has stopped me
in my over-achieving tracks,
I pause in awe of the miracle I have been given,
the miracle I dare not take for granted.

As I try to sit still and recover,
may I hear with clarity and gratitude
the word predestined to start this chapter,
the word the spirit whispers to me in earnest,
Wait.

Seek, Wait, Trust

But our citizenship is in heaven. And we eagerly await a savior from there, the Lord Jesus Christ, who, by the power that enables him to bring everything under his control, will transform our lowly bodies so that they will be like his glorious body. – Philippians 3:20-21

Altered Awareness

I have been put
Through another refining fire
And forged
Or more accurately
Forced
To look at my own mortality
In a fresh new way
That makes me inexpressibly joyful.

How can I possibly find words
To reveal just how grateful I am
To be alive?
May my altered awareness
Enable me
To lovingly experience
A life-embracing
Authentic existence.

On such a journey of faith,
May I fully view
Taking time to heal
As an opportunity
To draw closer
To God's greatest gift,
His Son, the Lord Jesus Christ,
Whose coming I await.

Wait Steadfastly

Create in me a pure heart, O God, and renew a steadfast spirit within me. – Psalm 51:10

Waiting Patiently

As a child,
many a Christmas morning
I waited impatiently with my siblings
for our aunt and uncle to arrive,
so we could open the sliding
wooden doors that barred
our view of the living room.
A childless couple,
they were unaware of the anxiety
and fidgeting this created in us.
There were more than visions
of sugar plums dancing in our heads!

As time dragged on,
my mother yearly pronounced,
"Patience is a virtue"
to our pouting faces.
Such wisdom fell on deaf ears.
We knew in that forbidden room
the fireplace would be lit,
overstuffed stockings would be hung,
a tree sparkling with ornamental majesty
would have magically appeared overnight,
and the presents we had asked Santa
to bring would be prominently displayed.

As an adult,
I'm sometimes like that over-anxious child,
trying to wrestle
my desired answer from the Lord.
Remembering "patience is a virtue"
still doesn't always help.
A steadfast spirit is renewed
only after waiting patiently.
Stubborn selfishness
must be struck down,
until I grasp
God is purifying my heart.

Seek, Wait, Trust

He says, "Be still, and know that I am God; I will be exalted among the nations, I will be exalted in the earth." – Psalm 46:10

Be Still

I want you to *be still*
and know that I am God.
In your haste,
doing what you deem important,
you miss precious time with me.

Today you woke with a start
in a house
as quiet as a sunrise.
Why not wait with me
for the dawn of a new day?

Before the coffee starts brewing
or the first chirp of the morning lark,
quiet your spirit
and feel my presence.
My love is real.

Avoid fretting about the past
or worrying about the future.
Meet me right here,
right now.
Be still and know that I am God.

At the time I have decided, my words will come true. You can trust what I say about the future. It may take a long time but keep on waiting, it will happen! – Habakkuk 2:3 (CEV)

Look Fully at the Lord

Love yourself and others
Simply because Jesus loves you deeply,
But take your eyes off yourself;
Look fully at the Lord!
He leads.
He shapes.
He makes new.
It may take a long time but keep on waiting;
It will happen!
He will change you,
And you will hardly know it is happening.
He will give you patience,
Love,
Joy,
Peace.
Look to Jesus for answers.
He is your shepherd:
Follow his lead,
Do not struggle,
Just relax in the Lord's love.
God says, *You can trust what I say about the future.*
His love made known in Christ Jesus is sufficient.
Keep on waiting; the Lord will supply all your needs.
Allow Jesus to do his Father's will;
Let him make you his disciple.
Let his love flow from you, spilling over to all you touch.
Look to Jesus; see how he loves you!

Seek, Wait, Trust

What strength do I have, that I should still hope? What prospects, that I should be patient? Surely I spoke of things I did not understand, things too wonderful for me to know. – Job 6:11 & 42:3b

Heavy Fog

We often get discouraged too quickly.
Hopelessness and apathy settle in
like a heavy summer fog
over a copious cornfield.
We complain of our lot in life
to anyone who will listen.
Surely we speak of things
we do not understand,
things too wonderful
to comprehend on our own.
For if we truly believe
that God is in control
of our lives
and of his world,
we would wait patiently
for the fog to lift
and his will
and his way
to become
plainly
visible.

Just as people are destined to die once, and after that to face judgment, so Christ was sacrificed once to take away the sins of many people, and he will appear a second time, not to bear sin, but to bring salvation to those who are waiting for him. – Hebrews 9:27-28

The Path of Salvation

Oh, God,
creator of our bodies,
minds,
and souls,
in your infinite wisdom
you have seen
that we are not able to face
the final judgment
without a savior.
Our human errors
and sinful natures
fall short
of your goodness.

Christ has covered our sins
with his blood
at Calvary.
He has paid the ultimate price
to secure our place
in paradise.
We wait patiently
for him,
because none of us
deserve to approach you
any way other
than the path
of salvation.

Seek, Wait, Trust

But for that very reason I was shown mercy so that in me, the worst of sinners, Christ Jesus might display his immense patience as an example for those who believe in him and receive eternal life. – I Timothy 1:16

Unlimited Patience

Sometimes a gentle hand
on our shoulder
from a spouse, friend, or relative
reminds us to be less impatient
and show more tolerance
toward an imperfect child
who is making the same mistake
over and over again.

That unsolicited touch
calms us,
allowing us to display patient kindness
rather than curt criticism.
Tender tugs to our restless agitation
allow God room to recreate
us in his own image
moment by moment.

On a much grander scale,
Jesus displays unlimited patience
with those on the bottom,
those without power,
those who have gone astray,
those seeking forgiveness.
He will come again to bring salvation
to those who are waiting for him.

Paul describes himself
as *the worst of sinners*.
Yet, the risen Savior turns his life around
and makes him a true apostle.
My sins are often caused by character flaws
on continuous loop.
Gratefully, Jesus displays *immense
patience* with me, as well.

Wait Steadfastly

We wait in hope for the LORD; he is our help and our shield. In him our hearts rejoice, for we trust in his holy name. May your unfailing love be with us, LORD, even as we put our hope in you. – Psalm 33:20-22

Waiting in Hope

I once waited uncomfortably with my grandma
As she placed a bet at the racetrack.
Later, we watched her chosen horse enter the stall to prepare for the race.
I anxiously wondered, "Is he really powerful,
Or is he bucking his head in defiance?"
When the bell rang to start the race, Grandma asked,
"Is that our horse, #7, who came out at full speed?"
I let her know he was in the lead.
"Good. That makes him the pacesetter.
Let's pray he doesn't bobble."
I didn't think we should pray about a horse's ability to win, but I kept quiet.
"We need him to stay the course and not be a short runner.
Let's hope he's still in it to win it as he nears the finish line!
Is he following the jockey's commands?"
I didn't know the answer, so I shrugged my shoulders.
With a last burst of energy, #14 pulled ahead to win
And accepted the wreath of victory.
Then Grandma whispered, "Only bet on a sure thing."

I'd sooner *wait in hope for the Lord*;
Rather than earthly riches, I seek heavenly rewards.
Even when I'm needlessly backed into a corner
And others are restlessly wondering whether to bet on me,
I can calmly relax for *he is my help and my shield*.
From the very start of my faith journey,
My heart has rejoiced in you, Lord.
I truly trust in your lead.
Your *unfailing love* sets the pace.
If my faith ever wobbles,
I remember my victory has already been claimed
Through your son Jesus. Hallelujah!
Even when I am tempted to quit or my energy is waning,
I know in order to reach the final finish line
I must put my faith in you.
It is only because of your grace,
A crown of glory awaits.
Then I'll shout, "I'm glad I bet on a sure thing...the Lord Almighty!"

Seek, Wait, Trust

Therefore, as God's chosen people, holy and dearly loved, clothe yourselves with compassion, kindness, humility, gentleness and patience. – Colossians 3:12

Founded Fears

Lord, I feel for the children…
The child who does not learn to read,
The one in poverty and need;
The child responsible for younger kin,
The one who bleakly knows he'll never win;
The child whose anger daily shows,
The one whose feelings no one knows;
The child with terror written on her face,
The one whose innocence has been erased;
The child fleeing the war-torn country of their birth,
The one who sadly feels unwelcome on the earth.
The child who can no longer cry,
The one who can't even ask why.
In their sorrow…
I sense humanity's callous inequities.

Lord, I weep for the children…
In their helpless inexperience,
In their increasing indifference;
In their restrained retrospect,
In their flippant disrespect;
In their hopeless ignorance,
In their wrathful violence;
In their weakened belief in you,
In their diminished point of view;
In their repressed anger,
In their darkest despair;
In their founded fears,
In their unseen tears.
In their heartache…
I witness the world's widening inhumanity.

Wait Steadfastly

Lord, I pray for the children...
Let their true worth daily be respected
And their precious lives be protected.
Let them know *compassion* as they each grow
And are nurtured in body, mind, and soul.
Let there be an end to war and violence,
So we can protect their childish innocence.
Let their frustrations safely be released
And their role models be people of peace.
Let them humbly find their way to you;
May your grace and love form them anew.
Let them be filled with faith-based assurance
As they learn loving *kindness* and *patience*.
In our gentle care for or brutal mistreatment of children...
I see society's future restoration or demise.

Yet the Lord longs to be gracious to you; he rises to show you compassion. For the Lord is a God of justice. Blessed are all who wait for him! – Isaiah 30:18

Your Graciousness

Alone,
struggling with self-pity,
I have shouted in utter frustration,
"Why is this happening to me?
That was so hateful.
I don't deserve this.
Life is so unfair!"

For generations, God has answered
such cries through the Holy Word
For the Lord is a God of justice;
Blessed are all who wait for him!
The Lord continually cautions,
"Act justly, love mercy,
and walk humbly with (me)."*

At my lowest moments,
I have sobbed,
"Lord, I need to feel your touch,"
and you have wrapped me
in your arms
like a soothing mother
calming her crying child.

In sickness and in sadness,
I wait for your solace, O Lord.
Longing *to be gracious* to me,
you brush the side of my cheek
with a tender stroke
of your compassionate hand.
I am comforted by your love.

---

* Micah 6:8

Wait for the gift my Father promised which you heard me speak about. For John baptized with water, but in a few days you will be baptized with the Holy Spirit. – Acts 1:4b-5

A Close Encounter

One afternoon,
while picnicking alone on the beach,
about ten seagulls
descended on me,
snatching my chips from the blanket
and my half-eaten sandwich from my hand.
I laughed and said,
"You're welcome,"
to my intruders.

I think of that unique experience
when I hear the phrase,
"The Holy Spirit descended on them like a dove."
Perhaps a dove swooping down
is calmer than those seagulls.
Even so,
as exciting as a Holy Ghost encounter might be,
like trying to stand upright in a windstorm,
it must be laced with fear as well.

Flushed with joy
as noticeable
as Pentecostal tongues of fire,
filled with the glory of God,
at one with the universe,
united in one accord
with brothers and sisters in Christ,
empowered with holy boldness,
what a life-changing moment that would be!

Seek, Wait, Trust

Since you have kept my command to endure patiently, I will also keep you from the hour of trial that is going to come upon the whole world to test those who live on earth. – Revelations 3:10

Firmly Focused

The long-distance runner
knows how to pace herself:
starting out strong,
patiently enduring the aches and pains
along the journey,
keeping her mind's eye
firmly focused
on the finish line,
saving a sudden burst of strength
and stamina
to sprint
ahead
of her contenders.

Is she running a similar race
in the spiritual realm?
Will she start out strong
but get easily sidetracked
by past problems
or future fears?
Does she know how to patiently endure
life's many challenges and obstacles?
She must maintain a moral fortitude
and develop a humble heart
to face the trials ahead
and win
the ultimate race.

Be patient, then brothers and sisters, until the Lord's coming. See how the farmer waits for the land to yield its valuable crop and how patient he is for autumn and spring rains. You, too, be patient and stand firm, because the Lord's coming is near. – James 5:7-8

Cultivating Patience

A farmer
Knows all about patience.
After careful planning,
He prepares the soil,
Plants the seeds,
Waters his fields and prays for spring rain,
Leaving his worries with the Creator.
Later he pulls the weeds,
Prunes and pampers the plants
And waits
Expectantly for the autumn harvest.

Christians, likewise,
Need to cultivate patience
While preparing for *the Lord's coming*.
They should plant seeds of righteousness,
Nurturing the Spirit faithfully
With daily devotions and prayers.
Firmly they must weed out faults and fears,
Pruning away character defects
Like arrogance, anger, or envy,
While calmly waiting
Until God gathers the crop in due season.

Seek, Wait, Trust

The Lord is not slow in keeping his promise, as some understand slowness. He is patient with you, not wanting anyone to perish, but everyone to come to repentance. – II Peter 3:9

In Need of Humbling

"Maybe God isn't done
humbling you yet,"
was what my friend had said.
What I heard instead was,
"Maybe God isn't done
humbling him yet."

I nodded in agreement,
hugged her,
said goodbye and drove off,
counting all the ways
my ex-husband needed
to get his act together.

Halfway home
the pronoun differences
hit me.
She thought
I was the one
who still needed humbling!

Those convicting words
reverberated in my head,
like a booming cymbal
hit at unexpected moments,
for days and months
and years.

Wait Steadfastly

Today
I heard those words
like a mantra in my head.
I had to sigh
contritely
at my continued arrogance.

After apologizing to the one I had unintentionally hurt,
I humbly bowed before the Lord
to ask for forgiveness.
I always find him patiently waiting
for me to get over my self-delusion.
Truly God isn't done humbling me yet!

Seek, Wait, Trust

Listen to my words, Lord, consider my lament. Listen to my cry for help, my King and my God, for to you I pray. In the morning, Lord, you hear my voice; in the morning I lay my requests before you and wait expectantly. – Psalm 5:1-3

In the Morning Stillness

In the morning stillness,
I whisper your name, O Lord.
Before I even get out of bed,
I say a thank you
for giving me another day
to live life to its fullest.

In the morning stillness,
I cry for help.
I know you listen.
The sadness in my heart
over my loved one's recent death
lessens when shared with you.

In the morning stillness,
there is no need for instant answers.
You are the divine artist.
I trust each stroke of your brush
for you create beauty out of ugly situations,
growth out of pain, and joy out of sorrow.

In the morning stillness,
you hear my voice…
I lay my requests before you
and wait expectantly.
I know your ultimate answer
will be what is best for all concerned.

In the morning stillness,
praise comes easy.
The sunbeams dance
to the song the nearby birds are chirping.
All living creatures join the joyful chorus.
The earth is full of humble adoration.

Wait Steadfastly

In the morning stillness,
I delight in your presence, O Lord.
The sound of my breath
echoes the beat of my heart.
I know you are as close as that heartbeat,
as real as the air I breathe.

We do not want you to become lazy, but to imitate those who through faith and patience inherit what has been promised. – Hebrews 6:12

Imitating Faith in Action

To imitate faith in action,
try to demonstrate
the willingness of Sarah
as she bore children at an old age,
the trust of Abraham
when he placed Isaac on the altar,
or the obedience of Moses
as he confronted Pharaoh.

Strive for the endurance of Joshua
when he survived the battle of Jericho,
the devotion of Ruth
as she stood by her mother-in-law,
the accountability of Esther
whose family would have perished without her,
or the patience of Job
as he faced yet another trial.

Pray for the perseverance of David
when he was forced into exile in the desert,
the loyalty of Jonathan
as he protected his friend and mentor,
the wisdom of Solomon
when he wrote such profound proverbs,
or the vision of Isaiah
as he unveiled God's salvation.

Feign the fearlessness of Jeremiah
when he lashed out at his contemporaries,
the courage of Daniel
as he endured the lion's den,
the righteousness of Amos
when he called for social justice,
or the faithfulness of Mary
as she submitted to the Holy Spirit.

Wait Steadfastly

Show the sincerity of the widow
as she surrendered her entire savings,
the honesty of the woman at the well
when she admitted her immorality,
the calm assurance of Abigail
when she stood up to an approaching army,
or the empathy of John
as he comforted Mary at the foot of the cross.

Replicate the receptiveness of Paul
whose life turned around on the road to Damascus,
the humility of Peter
as he faced martyrdom,
the trustworthiness of Timothy
when he helped the early churches,
or the compassion of Christ
as he was crucified for our sins.

With such patience modeled
by the Son of God
and by men and women of faith,
there is no room
for spiritual laziness,
especially
if we truly want to inherit
the kingdom of heaven!

Seek, Wait, Trust

I waited patiently for the Lord; he turned to me and heard my cry. He lifted me out of the slimy pit, out of the mud and mire; he set my feet on a rock and gave me a firm place to stand. He put a new song in my mouth, a hymn of praise to our God. – Psalm 40: 1-3a

God Alone Saves

Safety is a big concern
in our culture.
Schools, airports, court houses,
museums, and stadiums
require a security check.
We can't even enter
some emergency wards
without being wanded.
Are we really safe,
or are we living
under an illusion of safety?

Are we as serious
about protecting our spiritual life?
When we call on the Lord,
he helps us avoid danger.
He gives his protection
when we patiently
wait for him.
His gift of grace brings salvation
through faith in his son Jesus
whose very name means
"God saves."

Turn to God always.
He sees each tear drop;
he hears every cry.
All the overwhelming obstacles
life puts in our way,
God can overcome.
He offers us firm footing
in every circumstance,
if we are walking with him.
Sing his praises;
God alone saves.

Be completely humble and gentle, be patient, bearing with one another in love. Make every effort to keep the unity of the spirit through the bond of peace. – Ephesians 4:2-3

Gentle Thoughts

Sometimes
we are as different
as December and July.
Communication gaps
exasperate our arguments.
We start getting defensive
and stop listening.

If either or both of us
get arrogant or rude,
irritated, impatient,
or hateful,
the haze of hurtful harm
seems as acidic
as a Kaffir lime.

The wise way
to be united
in spirit
is to peacefully coexist
with Christ-like compassion,
*bearing with one another
in love.*

I can't change you;
I can only change myself.
In my morning meditations,
may I muster up
more humility
until my thoughts are as gentle
as a grandmother's lullaby.

Help me, Lord.
Quiet my fears.
Slow my heartbeat.
Calm my anxious spirit
until I can patiently respond
with consideration
and kindness.

Seek, Wait, Trust

> *I wait for the Lord; my whole being waits, and in his word I put my hope.*
> *I wait for the Lord more than the watchmen wait for the morning,*
> *more than the watchmen wait for the morning.* – Psalm 130:5-6

Valuable

Hazelnut coffee,
blending with the pine scent
of the surrounding forest,
warms away the chill
of the mountaintop's crisp,
clean air.

The early morning
dew seeps
through the blanket
on which I perch.
Twigs snap
in the stillness.

Three white-tailed deer
diverted by the plaintive sound
of a dove
retreat to the East
where a tiny fleck of red
appears on the horizon.

Streaks
of pinks
and purples,
with golden hues,
begin to sparkle
off the lake below.

Colors ignite
soundless
fireworks.
I whisper,
*The world is charged
with the grandeur of God.*[5]

Wait Steadfastly

Peering over the shoulder
of an artist
sketching a masterpiece,
I have caught a glimpse
of God
at his creative best.

As sunlight overtakes the sky,
I sense my insignificant.
"Yet I am valuable,"
my stirring soul seems to whisper,
"because I am God's creation, too."
Never have I felt his presence closer.

Seek, Wait, Trust

Praise be to the God and Father of our Lord Jesus Christ, the Father of compassion and the God of all comfort, who comforts us in all our troubles, so that we can comfort those in trouble with the comfort we ourselves receive from God. For just as we share abundantly in the sufferings of Christ, so also our comfort abounds through Christ. If we are distressed, it is for your comfort and salvation; if we are comforted, it is for your comfort, which produces in you patient endurance of the same sufferings we suffer. – II Corinthians 1:3-6

Overflowing Compassion

When we lay our troubles,
Our anxieties and fears,
Our world-weary wounds,
Our deepest disappointments
Our selfish greed
And especially our errant sins
At the foot of the cross,
Jesus brings comfort,
Rest and forgiveness.

As we patiently endure
The challenges we face in life,
Let us remember
To also lift in prayer
Others in distress…
For Christ's overflowing compassion
Covers them as well.
Reflecting on God's grace,
We discover our common humanity.

We are then able to offer
Christ-like comfort to others.
Sometimes it's as simple as a phone call,
Or as profound as being the first
One there after the death of a loved one,
Or the lifeline bringing food
Where there is none.
Always it means bringing hope
When all seems lost.

The creation waits in eager expectation for the children of God to be revealed. – Romans 8:19

Eager Expectation

Our ancient ancestors
wisely waited for centuries
for the arrival
of the Messiah,
the anointed one.
Now we,
followers of Jesus,
continue that vigil—
awaiting his promised return
with ardent anticipation.
May we be filled
with the spirit of love
his earlier arrival brought
For we strive to be among those
who share in Christ's eternal glory.

Just as we know
spring will eventually come
no matter how gray, dirty and depressing
the end of winter can be,
so *creation waits*
in eager expectation
for the children of God to be revealed.
Like crocuses and daffodils dancing,
pure joy will embody believers
during Christ's second coming.
In the meantime,
may we be filled with sure gratitude
for the wonderous ways
our Savior's saving teachings are woven
into the fabric of our daily lives.

Seek, Wait, Trust

Be joyful in hope, patient in affliction, faithful in prayer. – Romans 12:12

You Alone

I have been estranged from a loved one
For far too long.
Although there's a giant hole in my heart,
If I patiently put my hope in you, Lord,
I can still be joyful despite the sadness.
I know, as the Prince of Peace,
The God of love,
The Spirit of truth and justice,
You alone can bring reconciliation;
You alone shall still my over-anxious soul.

As long-suffering as Job, if need be,
I will unwaveringly trust in you, Lord.
Provide me with the patience
Of the prodigal's father.
He waited years for his son's return.
His unconditional love never vacillated.
Keep me steadfast and faithful in prayer,
For you alone know the outcome.
You alone
Can bring my loved one home.

But you must return to your God, maintain love and justice, and wait for your God always. – Hosea 12:6

Return to God

It's easy to make excuses
and imagine we're always right.
Courage will uncover our faults,
wisely banishing them from sight.

God offers us a better way;
looking at our imperfections
will help us understand our fears,
failures and daily frustrations.

To change, we must return to God.
Rising early to start each day,
spending quiet time with the Lord,
we'll strive to meditate and pray.

Knowing he listens to patient,
persistent, soul-searching prayer,
we will stop dreading the future
or reliving the past's harsh lair.

Seeking to follow God's guidance,
we'll learn to be loving and just.
Waiting for God to restore us,
we'll discern what it means to trust.

Seek, Wait, Trust

A patient man has great understanding, but a quick-tempered man displays folly. A hot-tempered man stirs up dissension, but a patient man calms a quarrel. – Proverbs 14:29 & 15:18

Choosing Words Wisely

A patient man has great understanding,
but a quick-tempered man displays folly.
The former is sweet-mannered
and chooses his words wisely.
The latter self-righteously
spews out anger without forethought.
One is stable, sensitive,
and as passive as a loyal golden retriever
lying faithfully at his master's feet.
The other can be as unstable, insensitive,
and aggressive as a suddenly violent pit bull
disloyally attacking a defenseless child.

A hot-tempered man stirs up dissension,
but a patient man calms a quarrel.
The former hatefully
and senselessly destroys relationships.
The latter lovingly
and wisely builds community.
One is critical, demeaning,
and as difficult as a world-worn alley cat
rebelliously instigating a street fight,
while the other is as loving, affirming
and easy to cherish as a newly rescued kitten
contentedly purring in a comforting lap.

Be still before the Lord and wait patiently for him; do not fret when people succeed in their ways, when they carry out their wicked schemes. Refrain from anger and turn from wrath; do not fret – it leads only to evil. For those who are evil will be destroyed, but those who hope in the Lord will inherit the land...Hope in the Lord and keep his way. – Psalm 37:7-9, 34a

A Rainbow of Hope

Be still.
Time alone with the Lord
is a breathtaking rainbow of hope
peeking through anxiety
and fears with flashes
of colorful wonder.

Wait patiently.
God's awe-filled grandeur
doesn't need water droplets
or a certain time of day to manifest his presence.
Discover him here and now…
as real as air.

Do not fret.
Amidst the rainstorms of life,
the Creator's covenant is made known.
His son streams through clouds of doubt.
Come full circle
back to the true source of strength.

Refrain from anger. Turn from wrath.
Form a rainbow coalition
of inclusive friendships.
The Heavenly Father is the God
of peace and serenity
and all-embracing love.

Hope in the Lord.
His rainbow rays reflect life,
healing, sunlight, nature, harmony, and spirit.
Hold on to God's promises.
Ultimately, he will right all wrongs.
Find joy in just being still in his presence.

Seek, Wait, Trust

Love is patient, love is kind. It does not envy, it does not boast, it is not proud. It does not dishonor others, it is not self-seeking, it is not easily angered, it keeps no record of wrongs. Love does not delight in evil but rejoices with the truth. It always protects, always trusts, always hopes, always perseveres. – I Corinthians 13:4-7

Love Is Patient

In divorce court,
it is easy to see
when love has left a marriage.
The couple is impatient,
unkind to each other,
resentful, rude, and arrogant.
Each insists,
"I am the injured party,
the one telling the truth."

In a sound relationship,
it is necessary
to strive to keep love alive.
Partners must be patient,
kind and comforting to one another,
accepting, respectful, and humble.
Both vow
to be affirming
and trustworthy.

Spiritually,
it is necessary to center
on the Lord to learn
love is faithful,
hopeful and caring.
It is not selfish or easily angered.
A Christian couple who pledges
to loyally love God and each other
protects their enduring union.

A man's wisdom gives him patience; it is his glory to overlook an offense. – Proverbs 19:11

Another Way

The teacher
who patiently shows
her perplexed pupil
yet another way,
rather than a flash
of indignant frustration,
builds a passageway
from present
confusion
to future
understanding.

God teaches us
to avoid the foolishness
of a lost temper
and the dissension it causes.
We must repeatedly learn
to overlook minor offenses
and sincerely show compassion.
Patience perfects
and guides us
along the path
to wisdom.

Seek, Wait, Trust

Do not say, "I'll pay you back for this wrong!" Wait for the Lord, and he will deliver you."
– Proverbs 20:22 (CEV)

This calls for patient endurance and faithfulness on the part of the saints. – Revelations 13:10b

Put in Perspective

In the book
of Revelations,
John called for
patient endurance
and faithfulness
on the part of the saint
even if that meant persecution,
being held captive,
exiled on a desolate island,
or killed
standing up for their faith.

Put in perspective,
we should be especially grateful
for the religious freedom
we often take for granted,
even when that means
waiting steadfastly
for God to make his will
and his way known to us.
Afterall, it is our needs,
not our wants,
he promises to fulfill.

We know how to wait
for trains, planes, and vacations.
We are herded into crowded arenas
and amusement parks for hours on end.
Drastic life changes may breed more patience
and tame our curt irritation with delay,
but has our faith in God remained intact?
King Solomon with ancient wisdom cautions,
Do not say, "I'll pay you back for this wrong!"
Wait for the Lord, and he will deliver you."
Truly it is the Lord who will help us endure.

Yet I will wait patiently for the day of calamity to come . . . though the fig tree does not bud and there are no grapes on the vines, though the olive crop fails and the fields produce no food, though there are no sheep in the pen and no cattle in the stalls, yet I will rejoice in the Lord. I will be joyful in God my savior. The sovereign Lord is my strength. – Habakkuk 3:16b-19

Rejoice in the Lord

Imagine having a spirit swift as a deer
so you could confidently leap out of harm's way
or jump to new heights of awareness or service,
running life's rapid race with endless endurance.

Picture having a seasoned farmer's patience.
He believes God helps through any calamity—
floods, hurricanes, tornadoes, droughts, infestations—
knowing failed crops are followed by fruitful seasons.

Envision having a firm faith like Habakkuk
who daily conversed with and waited for the Lord.
He bravely counseled Daniel in the lion's den,
sharing strength that could only come from God.

Experience having a new believer's joy
so you can rejoice in the Lord no matter what...
in good times and in bad, in plenty and in loss,
waiting patiently for God's will to work out well.

Seek, Wait, Trust

But if we hope for what we do not yet have, we wait for it patiently...we know that in all things God works for the good of those who love him, who have been called according to his purpose. – Romans 8:25, 28

Answering God's Call

One God.
One faith.
One baptism.
A long-awaited desire
to draw closer
to our maker.

One way.
One truth.
One life.
A savior who
can wash away
the sin of the world.

One thought.
One belief.
One hope:
that in all things
God works for the good
of those who love him.

One day.
One moment.
One leap of faith
as we each answer
God's call
to love.

For the grace of God that brings salvation has appeared to all. It teaches us to say, "No" to ungodliness and worldly passions and to live self-controlled, upright and godly lives in this present age, while we wait for the blessed hope – the glorious appearing of our great God and Savior, Jesus Christ, who gave himself for us, to redeem us from all wickedness and to purify for himself a people that are his very own, eager to do what is good. – Titus 2: 11-14

Forever Changed

There are people
who come into our lives,
changing us
for the better.

They have a larger-than-life
influence on us,
bolstering our fragile
self-esteem.

Jesus has that power.
He radically reshapes lives.
Following his lead,
we improve day by day.

He inspires
and saves us,
sacrificing his own life
to forgive our sinful ways.

Our great God
graces us with the gift of his son,
encouraging our eagerness
to do good.

We wait with *blessed hope*
for the Lord's return,
longing to be
forever changed.

Seek, Wait, Trust

The fruit of the Spirit is love, joy, peace, patience, kindness, goodness, faithfulness, gentleness and self-control. – Galatians 5: 22

Fruitful

Lord, fill me with the spirit
of love
as abundant
as the grains of sand at the seashore,
of joy
as breath-taking
as a mountaintop panorama,
of peace
as serene
as a purple and pink sunset.

Lord, fill me with the spirit
of patience
as straight
as a path lined with poplar trees,
of kindness
as unfailing
as the morning sunrise,
of goodness
as dazzling
as a double rainbow.

Lord, fill me with the spirit
of faithfulness
as overflowing
as a forest waterfall,
of gentleness
as soothing as a summer breeze,
and of self-control
as respectable as a rippling river,
so that I might be as fruitful
as a field of favored grapevines.

The eyes of all look to you, and you give them their food at the proper time. You open your hand and satisfy the desires of every living thing. – Psalm 145:15-16

The Answer

It was years later,
but I knew
in the depths
of my soul
that God had answered
my inner-most longing.

His timing
was so perfect
that the word
"finally"
was the farthest thing
from my mind.

A total solar eclipse
may occur only
once in a decade,
but those who witness it
are awestruck
for a lifetime.

To know
God heard
my cry,
when it was barely audible,
is just as awe-inspiring
and life-affirming.

To realize he shaped
and formed me
over the years,
until I was finally ready
to fully appreciate his answer,
is even more miraculous!

Seek, Wait, Trust

Make me to know thy ways, O Jehovah; teach me thy paths. Make me to walk in thy truth and teach me: for thou art the God of my salvation; on thee do I wait all the day. – Psalm 25: 4-5 (DARBY)

His Guidance

As I patiently pray for pure peace of mind,
I must let go of my perfectionism,
For only God's love is the perfect prism.
I'll wait for his guidance—so truthfully kind.

His glow in the darkness is my paradigm.
Anxiety is calmed accepting God's will.
My fear is replaced by faith; my spirit is still.
He shows me what path to take following him.

My Savior is leading me in novel ways.
Belief in him precedes belief in myself.
I must put doubt and rejections on a shelf,
For God's love is sufficient all of my days.

I'll never forget the price of salvation,
A gift gracefully given by God to us.
Reflecting the Light of the world, Christ Jesus,
Illuminates my own daily devotion.

I might miss the miracles God has in mind
Unless I walk in his truth to help others,
Dispersing his love to sisters and brothers.
I'll wait for his guidance—so truthfully kind.

Rather as servants of God, we commend ourselves in every way: in great endurance; in hardships and distress; in beatings, imprisonments, and riots; in hard work, sleepless nights, and hunger; in purity, understanding, patience and kindness; in the Holy Spirit and in sincere love; in truthful speech, and in the power of God, with weapons of righteousness...and yet we live on: beaten and yet not killed; sorrowful yet always rejoicing; poor, yet making many rich; having nothing, yet possessing everything. – II Corinthians 6:4-10

Possessing Everything

I met a woman who was beaten
and disowned
by her family
and imprisoned
by her country
for becoming a Christian.
At great personal peril,
she fled to America
seeking political asylum
and religious freedom.
Her life here has not been easy.
She works three jobs
and still faces
loneliness,
discrimination,
and relentless
financial struggles,
but her face
radiates
an inner joy
unmatched
by anyone I know.
To me,
she personifies the words,
having nothing,
yet possessing everything.
Waiting
on the Lord
doesn't mean
we will get everything
we want,
but we will have everything
we need.

Seek, Wait, Trust

Only God can save me, and I calmly wait for him. – Psalm 62:1 (CEV)

As you know, we consider those who have persevered. You have heard of Job's perseverance and have seen what the Lord finally brought about. The Lord is full of compassion and mercy. – James 5:11

Put to the Test

No one
Wants to be put to the test
Like Job.
It may feel like we are being tested now.

Remember Job survived loss after loss,
Pain on top of pain,
Trial trailing trial.
Our faith will help us endure present hardships.

God valued Job's righteous suffering
Just as he uses our daily struggles to sanctify us.
Pray for perseverance,
Waiting with a grateful heart for this to pass.

The Lord is full of compassion and mercy.
Do not fear;
God helps us through times of trouble.
He will not leave us alone.

Only God
Can save us,
And we calmly
Wait for him.

I pray that God will be kind to you and will bless you with peace! We thank God for you and always mention you in our prayers. Each time we pray, we tell God our Father about your faith and loving work and about your firm hope in our Lord Jesus Christ. —My dear friends, God loves you, and we know he has chosen you to be his people. Everyone is talking about how you welcomed us and how you turned away from idols to serve the true and living God. They also tell how you are waiting for his Son Jesus to come from heaven. God raised him from death, and on the day of judgment Jesus will save us from God's anger. – I Thessalonians 1:1-4, 9-10 (CEV)

Laced with Excitement

Apprehension laced with excitement and fear
Surround the beginning of many things…
Learning to ride a bike or play a musical instrument,
The start of a new school year or a new job,
Adolescence and adulthood,
A much-anticipated change or a forthcoming move,
Marriage or the birth of a baby.

Apprehension laced with excitement and fear
Surround the end of many things…
Perhaps childhood,
Elementary school, middle school, high school or college,
A task, an exam, or a pivotal performance,
A failing relationship or impending divorce,
A devastating storm or even life itself.

Even though we know Jesus is the beginning and the end,
Apprehension over his second coming
Is also laced with apprehension and fear.
It could be today, tomorrow, or in the near or distant future.
Yet, recent fires, floods, tornados and hurricanes,
The pandemic, and wars have everyone on edge,
Imminently waiting for *Jesus to come from heaven*.

Do not fear – we are his *chosen people*; his love is available always.
He still has *loving work* for us to do here on earth:
Serve the true and loving God, fostering his justice and goodness;
Walk with steadfast faithfulness, waiting for our Savior's return;
Share God's love with others, acting compassionately;
Welcome the stranger, longing to be fed in body and soul;
And go in peace, passing on Christ's message of mercy and healing.

Seek, Wait, Trust

Come to me all you who are weary and burdened and I will give you rest. Take my yoke upon you and learn from me, for I am gentle and humble of heart, and you will find rest for your souls. – Matthew 11:28-29

Rest

Come to me all you who are weary and burdened,
And I will give you rest.
God knows you are drowning in responsibilities...
To your family, friends and loved ones.
You spend most waking hours working,
Leaving little time for things that truly matter.
Even your pursuit of happiness has brought fatigue.
You have forgotten true happiness dwells in unity
With your Lord and Savior.

Take my yoke upon you and learn from me,
For I am gentle and humble of heart.
That requires silence and waiting.
Take time to mediate as well as pray.
Repress your thoughts
Long enough to hear the guidance of the Holy Spirit.
Jesus, your Redeemer, has much to teach you
About love and loving...
The true meaning of life.

And you will find rest for your souls.
Breathe out the troubles of this world;
Breathe in the Lord's goodness and mercy.
Devote time for daily devotions;
That is a devout act of love.
Find relief in persistent, consistent prayer.
God, with the infinite patience
Of the only perfect parent,
Will provide the solace your spirit seeks.

Whatever is true, whatever is noble, whatever is right, whatever is admirable—if anything is excellent or praiseworthy—think about such things. Whatever you have learned or received or heard from me—put into practice. And the God of peace will be with you. – Philippians 4:8-9

Restored Confidence

Persevering in faith
Need not be as terrifying
As learning to ride a bike.

At first, you wobble back and forth
Between patience and frustration
Waiting to uncover God's perfect plan for you.

Sometimes you will wander off the path
Or fall scraping your ego.
You may even cry out in pain or aggravation.

God sent his son
To pick you up and comfort you.
Jesus cleans your bruises and redirects your course.

The Spirit within you renews your courage
As your faith and confidence are restored.
Eventually life's training wheels can be removed.

Fellow believers will cheer you on
Shouting, "Way to go! Praise the Lord!
We knew you could do it!"

God whispers, *Whatever you have learned*
Or received
Or heard from me—put into practice.

Always remember *the God of peace*
Will be with you along the way.
That is truly *excellent* and *praiseworthy*.

Seek, Wait, Trust

When God made his promise to Abraham, since there was no one greater for him to swear by, he swore by himself saying, "For I will surely bless you and give you descendants." And so after waiting patiently, Abraham received what was promised. – Hebrews 6: 13-15

Our Gracious God

Abraham and Sarah had to wait
Until old age
To be blessed
With a child.
God ultimately
Kept his promise.
Sarah threw her head back
And laughed uncontrollably
After being told
That the Lord,
To whom she had prayed for decades,
Had decided to deliver
A descendant after all.
His oath to her husband,
Despite the human improbability,
Was totally trustworthy.
We would do well
To learn from their story
And never give up
On our gracious God.
His perfect timing
Will delight us as well.

We know that all creation is still groaning and is in pain, like a woman about to give birth. The Spirit makes us sure about what we will be in the future. But now we groan silently, while we wait for God to show that we are his children. This means that our bodies will also be set free. And this hope is what saves us. But if we already have what we hope for, there is no need to keep on hoping. However, we hope for something we have not yet seen, and we patiently wait for it. – Romans 8:22-25 (CEV)

Hope Abounds

For many mothers,
The nine months of anticipation
Anxiously awaiting the birth of their child
May have been preceded by years of longing.
The groans of childbirth,
The most primal of screams,
Bear witness
To the pain radical change causes.
But *hope* abounds.
It is the expectation
Of a healthy
Longed-for
Loved one
That sees a new mother
Through the natural,
Or sometimes medically unnatural,
Birthing process.

For people of faith
Eagerly approaching eternal life,
Their impending crown of glory
May be preceded by a deep *groaning*.
Yet, the calm at a believer's deathbed
Replaces primal screams.
Confidence bears witness
To Christ's saving grace.
Such astounding *hope* abounds,
Born of belief in the unseen
And the ability to *patiently wait*
For final adoption into the family of God.
Serenity spreads over the loved one's countenance,
Now radiantly aglow with supernatural vision,
As an indisputable smile
In the face of death
Brings profound closure to the dying process.

Seek, Wait, Trust

The end of the matter is better than the beginning, and patience is better than pride. – Ecclesiastes 7:8

Knowledge Born of Patience

The end of the matter is better than the beginning.
Fond memories replace nerve-racking suspense.
Like an egret coasting effortlessly to a smooth landing,
Calm overcomes numbing nervousness.
Knowledge born of patient waiting for God-given guidance
Takes the place of panicked paranoid fear of the unknown.
Insular dread succumbs
To a sense of shared accomplishments,
And profound joy is even greater than anticipated excitement.

Patience is better than pride
For it is hopeful and kind rather than impatient and cruel.
A humble spirit-filled search for deep meaning and purpose
Far exceeds a life of boastful self-centeredness.
Smug vanity and selfish impatience are character flaws
Which can be overcome when anxiety-ridden arrogance
Is finally replaced with sweet serenity,
As poised as an undisturbed swan
Gliding gracefully on the surface of a crystal-clear pond.

But as for me, I watch in hope for the Lord. I wait for God my savior; my God will hear me. – Micah 7:7

The Winds of Change

Your love, O Lord, is the solar wind recharging our spirits.
Daily prayer and meditation help us recommit
To a life journey of drawing closer to you, for we must
Depend on your care in torrential times and learn to trust.

The storms which sometimes surround us can always be endured.
Patient prayers have produced faith that your answers are assured.
We have learned your way does not equal our selfish desires,
But the soothing breeze of your love is all each soul requires.

We pray this world will return to the one you created –
Where, living in peace, each person is no longer hated
For the color of their skin or cultural uniqueness.
Lord, hear our prayers wafting with gentle gusts of meekness.

Grant your guidance to help us weather change with confidence.
Our windswept lives need the shelter of your perfect presence.
Provide a flurry of strength and courage to do your will;
With Christ, we have a reconciling mission to fulfill.

Seek, Wait, Trust

"God opposes the proud but gives grace to the humble." Humble yourselves, therefore, under God's mighty hand, that he may lift you up in due time. Cast all your anxieties on him because he cares for you. And the God of all grace, who called you to his eternal glory in Christ, after you have suffered a little, will himself restore you and make you strong, firm and steadfast. – I Peter 5:6-7, 10

Along Life's Way

I used to assume my strong-willed determination
    was a life raft in a sea of despair;
now I realize, *God of all grace*,
    self-reliance makes me drift away from you.

I used to feel proud you had gifted me
    with intelligence and a talented flair;
now I have found, *Creator of all*,
    what you value most is humility.

I used to presume surrendering
    was incongruent with free will;
now I recognize, *steadfast Savior*,
    my stubbornness impedes your will.

I used to say, "Let go and let God,"
    but often impatient anxiety interfered;
now I've discovered, *compassionate Lord*,
    a calm serenity waiting with you.

I used to suppose I was weak,
    wavering and inconsistent;
now I've discerned, *Holy Spirit*,
    your comforting guidance restores my strength.

I used to wonder if you sent problems
    to test my faith along life's way;
now I've learned, *great reconciling God*,
    your grace allows growth to follow suffering.

Those who hope in the Lord will renew their strength. They will soar on wings like eagles; they will run and not grow weary; they will walk and not be faint...Since ancient times, no one has heard, no ear has perceived, no eye has seen any God besides you, who acts on behalf of those who wait for him – Isaiah 40:31; 64:4

Renewed Strength

There are people
    whose trials in life
are way beyond what most
    people can bear.
Perhaps he has survived a war,
    or she suffers silently with severe pain.
Some joyfully accept their life of poverty,
    or valiantly face
their last few hours of life
    with amazing grace and gratitude.

Those who hope in the Lord
    focus not on their current troubles
but on the endless faithfulness of their God
    who has brought them through
life's lingering challenges
    without weariness, without fainting.
They have learned *the Lord*,
    when asked,
will renew their strength
    to meet whatever comes next.

Do others who desperately need inner stamina
    also see God's grace glowing in us?
Despite earthly defeat
    is our *hope in the Lord?*
On wings like eagles,
    do we rise with faith above our troubles?
Do we know God brings good out of tribulation
    when we *wait for him?*
Then our spirits will shine as light in the darkness
    with the inner power of those we've admired!

Seek, Wait, Trust

Bear in mind that the Lord's patience means salvation. – II Peter 3:15a

Wait Steadfastly

When life is more than you can bear,

Accept the Lord's *salvation*.

Invite him into your life.

Tenderly and patiently, he will care for you.

Stop struggling and relax;

Trust that all will be well.

Each day will offer new light

Allowing you to see more clearly.

Dread will be replaced by hope.

Fear will give way to courage.

Acceptance will clear away the clouds of doubt.

Serenity will silence stress and anxiety.

Take time to rest in the Lord;

Let him supply all your needs.

You are his beloved child.

I remember my afflictions and my wandering, the bitterness and the gall. I well remember them, and my soul is downcast within me. Yet this I call to mind and therefore I have hope: Because of the Lord's great love we are not consumed, for his compassions never fail. They are new every morning; great is your faithfulness. I say to myself, "The Lord is my portion; therefore, I will wait for him." – Lamentations 3:19-24

Holy Happiness

In past and present trials,
What have I learned from waiting?
Through disappointments and challenges,
Woes and wayward wandering,
Trials and tribulations,
Mistakes and mishaps,
Sins and sorrows,
It is in you, Lord, *I have hope.*

You bought my salvation
At a heavy personal price.
You brought me from the brink
Of despair and self-destruction.
You taught me about unconditional love,
Allowing me to feel cherished
Despite how low I may have sunk.
It is in you, Lord, *I have hope.*

You lifted me out of self-pity,
Dusted off the layers
Of doubt and indifference,
And delivered me into the hands
Of caring, compassionate friends.
"Surely it was for my benefit
That I suffered such anguish."*
It is in you, Lord, *I have hope.*

Because of your great love, I have hope;
I am no longer confused.
Your consistent presence has healed
My wounded heart with holy happiness,
Permitting me to love you and others.
I will continue to wait on you,
Placing my trust in you.
Great is your faithfulness.

---

* Isaiah 38:17a

Seek, Wait, Trust

A WAITING PRAYER

Lord,

Bless now our time together in prayer. We thank you for another sun rising. We thank you for patiently watching over us through the night.

Help us to *be joyful in hope, patient in affliction, faithful in prayer.** Lord, tender our hearts to these words from your holy scripture that they may declare the righteousness and the justice and the goodness of the ministry of thy Son, Jesus Christ, our Lord, whose mission was about teaching and preaching and praying, healing, anointing, serving, and welcoming the gladness of the earth. Give us his patience and his prayerful connection with you so that we may observe and cheerily care for all you have created. Bless and touch the rivers and the seas, the land, and the air above. Bless the places where the foxes go and the birds nest, the homes that have been invaded by illness, the hospitals overrun by a new virus which has stricken the lives of so many and left others waiting and praying to be cured or spared.

Bless, Lord, the doctors, nurses, first responders, x-ray technicians, and medical assistants, and all those who work faithfully, yet fearlessly, in contact with something that might have a crucial bearing on their lives. In the midst of the current affliction, may they still find joy in their daily encounters with their patients.

Bless the House of leaders who make laws and declare the rulings of the government and who have the privilege of taking care of the citizens of these United States of America. May their hearts be filled with compassion. May the walls around each elected official's frozenness toward necessary legislation be melted. May their eyes see widely the hurt and pain of the people. May their ears hear the call of those crying out for food and money, a place to live, a job to go to work, a child to take care of, a baby to put diapers on, a mother to hold them close to her heart, and more than that, a father who accepts the responsibility and the accountability of loving his family the same way you love the children of Zion.

Bless, oh God, this day the uniqueness of the world that has come together with a globalized plea of justice and righteousness that Black Lives Matter. Yes,

---

* Romans 12:12

Lord, we echo that no life can matter in America until each black life matters. We also affirm that Christian lives matter, that Jewish lives matter, that Muslim lives matter...that children's lives matter, that women's lives matter, that men's lives matter...that the church matters, that each school matters, that people of all nations matter.

Lord, I pray that you will dispatch angels today from on high to look over the earth. In your Holy Word, you said you would dispatch 10,000 angels onto the mountainside to watch over the cattle and the herds and to go down by the stream to be amongst that which you made—mankind, just a little lower than the angels—to watch over this thy kingdom...the forests and the seas, the wilderness, and the entire earth.

So, be with us today, Lord, and in the weeks to come. Be with your people as we come to you daily in prayer: seeking to draw closer to you, laying our burdens before you, gratefully trusting in your amazing grace. Help us to wait patiently for the answers to our prayers and for the working out of your plans for each of us and for your Kingdom.

Now may the words of my mouth and the meditations of my heart be acceptable in thy sight, O God, my strength and my redeemer. Amen.

Watching over Us

CHAPTER 3:
TRUST COMPLETELY

Trusting the Way

But the Lord can be trusted to make you strong and protect you from harm. – II Thessalonians 3:3 (CEV)

God's Faithful Handiwork

Sometimes the Lord's presence
In our overwhelmed life
Takes on a miraculous form—
A cure when none is in sight,
Help from a stranger when we are lost and alone,
Escape from an impossible situation.
In the bleakest desert of our lives,
We find a baptismal pool.
Despite a whirlwind of fear surrounding us,
We feel an aura of light and love
Calming us.
Trusting the Lord
Gives us the strength
Needed to keep going.

We see God's faithful handiwork
In each precious newborn baby,
Especially in the birth of Mary's beloved son.
We spot the rainbow at the storm's end
Or sense the holy spirit burning in our bosom.
We feel the brush of an angel's wing
Against our quivering cheek
Or the Lord's loving hand on our shoulder
Reaching to gently guide our steps
Or calmly comfort us.
At times, as if through a dense cloud,
We hear the words of Scripture whisper,
*The Lord can be trusted to make you strong
and protect you from harm.*

Seek, Wait, Trust

In you, Lord my God, I put my trust. I trust in you; do not put me to shame, nor let my enemies triumph over me...I have trusted in the Lord and have not faltered...The Lord is my strength and my shield; my heart trusts in him, and he helps me. My heart leaps for joy, and with my song I praise him. – Psalm 25:1-2; 26:1b; 28:7

Radiating God's Love

I wish I could truthfully say,
*I have trusted in the Lord
And have not faltered.*
I do well when faced with trauma.
Wholeheartedly
I place my trust in God,
My protector who shields me
And helps me stay calm
As each tidal wave tries to crush me.

It's with little everyday challenges
That my consistency seems as shallow
As the last wave that laps the shoreline.
Forgetting where my true strength lies,
I sometimes dive into tedious tasks
Without a prayer or inspired insight,
Making matters worse instead of better.
I definitely need God's guidance
Overcoming day-to-day hurtles to my serenity.

I long for my devotion to reach ocean depth,
Replacing stubborn pride with humble prayers
And my anxieties with faith-filled assurance.
I'm purposely learning to leave all things
In God's almighty hands
To unequivocally live:
*The Lord is my strength and my shield.
My heart trusts in him,
And he helps me.*

Radiating God's love,
Like a mermaid glistening in the sunlight,
I wish to emerge each morning—
No longer spiritually adrift—
No matter how calm or troubled the waters.
Regardless of circumstances,
May I daily pause to ponder God's goodness
Until *My heart leaps for joy,
And with my song I praise him.*

In repentance and rest is your salvation, in quietness and trust is your strength. – Isaiah 30:15b

Jesus Knows

Jesus knows my spirit is willing,
But my body is weak.
Things of this world
Are wreaking havoc on my sensitive soul.
Jesus also observes the sorrow
That overwhelms me,
Making me lethargic
And paralyzed by doubt and fear.
He, too, was brought to his knees
By sadness.

When I turn my focus
From my own insecurities
Toward the compassionate
Eyes of my savior,
I truly see he feels my pain,
For he has suffered
Even to the point of death.
He reminds me,
In repentance and rest is your salvation,
in quietness and trust is your strength.

Through honest reflection,
Jesus moves me toward humility
Before the Lord.
I pray all night long, if need be,
Until "the peace of God,
Which transcends all understanding"*
Guards my heart and my thoughts.
God's plans for me become clearer.
My weary body finally feels refreshed,
And my spirit is renewed.

---

* Philippians 4:7

*Trust in the Lord with all your heart and lean not on your own understanding;
in all your ways acknowledge him,
and he will make your paths straight.* – Proverbs 3:5-6

A Straighter Path

I often
over-analyze things.
Unfortunately,
that doesn't always
make me right.
Like a biased research scientist
who stopped looking
beyond preconceived ideas,
I sometimes stick
to my original hypothesis
far too long.

I may even flit
from one fragmented thought
to another,
mistakenly thinking
concrete answers
will come
from my muddled brain.
My self-reliance
seems sane on the surface,
but such stubbornness
often leads me astray.

Yet, there is a wiser way...
placing my decisions and actions
before the Lord.
All that is false,
evil and damaging
will be sifted out.
The impossible
will become possible.
God will provide
a promising resolve
to a previously hopeless situation.

Trust Completely

As I seek spiritual sustenance
from holy scripture,
I clearly taste and see the solution:
Trust in the Lord
with all your heart
and lean not
on your own understanding.
In all your ways,
acknowledge him,
and he will make
your path straight.

Seek, Wait, Trust

> *I will wait for the Lord, who is hiding his face from the house of Jacob.*
> *I put my trust in him.* – Isaiah 8:17

Hide and Seek

I remember playing hide and seek with my dad
when I was little.
Just before he closed his eyes and started counting,
he saw tears in my eyes.
"What's wrong, sweetie?" he asked.

"What if you don't find me?" I sighed sheepishly.
"I'll keep looking until I do.
You're too special to leave lost and alone."
His comforting words gave me the courage
to run off and hide under my bed.

Closing my eyes,
I waited as he shouted out the last number and started his search.
I heard him say, "Where's my little one?
Where can she be?"
As he entered my room he whispered, "I wonder if I'm hot or cold?"

I giggled, cupping my hand over my mouth to quiet my heavy breathing.
Dad glanced in my direction.
Then he pretended to look in the closet,
the toy box and the dresser drawers,
but I knew he had already discovered my hiding place.

"What's this?" he said in mock surprise, "A shadow?
Why it looks like my little angel!"
Then he bent down and smiled at me.
Again, I giggled with glee
as he gently pulled me out and hugged me.

I hadn't panicked because I believed
he would seek me out and find me
no matter where I hid.
Even after covering his face,
he knew exactly where to find me.

God, too, always has me in His view.
He waits patiently when I hold back from Him...
busy with my hectic life
or overcome by emotions
or just seeking pleasure.

I spin and sin and hide
as pointlessly as Adam and Eve
when nakedly they hid
behind a tree
in the garden of Eden!

When I realize how dark my life is without God,
I shout out, "Help me, Lord.
Come find your lost lamb!"
He's already right there
for He knows my every need.

Isaiah waited on the Lord and trusted
In the one *hiding His face from the house of Jacob.*
As a result of that reliance on God,
Isaiah was able to predict key facts about Jesus
over seven hundred years before Christ's birth.

I want to stop hiding
and continue to spend my time seeking the Lord.
No matter how long I have to wait,
I know I will find Him by putting my trust
in the one whose face I cannot yet see.

Seek, Wait, Trust

But I will leave within you the meek and the humble, who trust in the name of the Lord. The remnant of Israel will do no wrong. They will speak no lies; nor will deceit be found in their mouths. They will eat and lie down, and no one will make them afraid. – Zephaniah 3:12-13

Pause to Ponder

Unlike an errant child expecting her parent
To straighten out her latest predicament,
I have struggled to leave my troubles
In your hands, Lord.

As soon as I lay my problems at your feet,
I pick them up again,
Put them right back in my pocket
And walk away from your guiding spirit.

Why do I think
I alone have the solutions
When clearly
You sent Jesus to show the way?

I find help with this internal struggle
In your Holy Word
Where you promise
Restoration to your remnant people.

Who you save gives me pause to ponder:
The meek and the humble;
The innocent few who tell the truth;
The fearless and the brave.

Lord, continue to humble me.
I want to live with authenticity
And sleep without fear,
Trusting all things to you.

When I am afraid, I will trust in you. In God, whose word I praise, in God I trust; I will not be afraid. What can mortal man do to me? In God, whose word I praise—in God I trust; I will not be afraid. What can man do to me? – Psalm 56: 3-4, 10-11

Protective Power

An insult swells in significance
Like a raised welt following a bee sting,
Overtaking my conscious thoughts,
Undercutting my inner peace.

Yet I'm the one who gives the words
The power to repeatedly prick me,
Replaying the phrases in my heart,
Wallowing in self-pity.

"No more!" I shout to my wounded ego.
Let me place this itching pain on the altar of prayer,
Experiencing God's protective power,
Shielding me against future attacks.

I recall a past abusive relationship
That was poisoned with potential danger.
My fears, back then, were raw and real.
But, just as tangible, was God's grace.

I will not be afraid for God is my strength.
Today's prayers will be a balm for my bruised ego,
Restoring my confidence,
Revitalizing my joyful spirit.

What can mortal man do to me?
In God, whose word I praise, I trust.
He defends me from all harm.
Then...now...always.

Seek, Wait, Trust

You are tempted in the same way that everyone else is tempted. But God can be trusted not to let you be tempted too much, and he will show you how to escape from your temptations. – I Corinthians 10:13 (CEV)

In your anger do not sin; when you are on your beds, search your hearts and be silent. Offer right sacrifices and trust in the Lord. – Psalm 4:4-5

The Light in the Darkness

God doesn't want us
to spend our lives
cowering in fear,
exasperated by anxiety;
nor does he want
our anger
to lead us
to sinful actions
that are
beneath us…

Instead, he asks us
to trust in him,
praying he will remove
our stubbornness,
our anger,
our self-centeredness,
our doubts,
our dread,
and any other self-defeating
character flaws.

When we silently
search our hearts,
we discover the Lord
can shine light
into such darkness
illuminating a path
that will give us
profound peace
and the calm assurance
that all will be well.

But I trust in you, Lord; I say, "You are my God. My times are in your hands; deliver me from the hands of my enemies, from those who pursue me. Let your face shine on your servant; save me in your unfailing love." – Psalm 31:14-16

Healing Hands

In our anger,
impatience, arrogance, and guilt,
we waste precious time
blaming others and pardoning ourselves.
Now is the time for humility
before our excesses and excuses draw us even further
from the calm, confident, competent children of God
we were created to be.
Nothing is ever solved hiding from the truth.

Striving to become better people,
we lean on the Lord who picks us up when we fall
and saves our lives from the ravages of sin.
We are miniscule in God's gigantic hand,
yet he gently strokes our fragile, broken wings
with unceasing compassion and undeserved forgiveness.
His arms protect, guide, and uphold us.
In the warmth of his tender care,
we begin to trust in his God-given grace.

Human hands can help or hurt,
create or tear down,
uplift with praise or point with blame,
gather or separate,
embrace with love or clench with hate,
reconcile or fight,
caress or kill.
God's healing hands from the beginning
have been creating all things good.

Once we learn
only God has the power
to redirect, reshape and restore us,
we can begin to face our shortcomings
with soul-searching honesty.
Daily we place our lives in his tender care.
Basking in the rays of his shining face,
we see a reflection of our perfected selves
in the light of his *unfailing* love.

Seek, Wait, Trust

Can papyrus grow tall where there is no marsh? Can reeds thrive without water? While still growing and uncut, they wither more quickly than grass. Such is the destiny of all who forget God. So perishes the hope of the Godless. What he trusts is fragile. – Job 18:11-14

Life without Trust

Life without trust in God
Is a spider web of lies
Intricately woven,
Seeming so real.
But each lie
Is fragilely
Built on the one
That precedes it.

Like the spider hanging
Precariously from the ceiling,
Life can be turned upside down,
And lies can be exposed
At any moment.
Anything,
Anyone
Can break the web.

Such is the destiny
Of all who forget God.
So perishes
The hope of the Godless.
What he trusts
Is fragile.
What she relies on
Is a spider web of lies.

Life with trust,
On the other hand,
Is woven with truth
And laced with God's grace.
"For his will is to be seen
And to be sought –
His will is to be waited for
And trusted."[6]

Surely God is my salvation; I will trust and not be afraid. The Lord, the Lord, is my strength and my song; he has become my salvation. With joy you will draw water from the wells of salvation. – Isaiah 12:2

Facing Tomorrow

You've cried.
You've screamed.
You've paced.
You've sobbed uncontrollably.

But, there's nothing you can do
About this problem
Tonight.
Close your eyes.

Quiet your spirit.
Breathe deeply.
Breathe in
The goodness of God.

Trust that he will
Get you through this.
Breathe out
Releasing your fears.

The Lord,
Your strength and your song,
Is also the source
Of your salvation and joy.

Like fresh water
From a mountain stream
He'll wash over you.
Your world

Weariness
Will be replaced with inner calm
And the power and courage
To face tomorrow.

Seek, Wait, Trust

He said to her, "Daughter, your faith has healed you. Go in peace, and be freed from your suffering."
– Mark 5:34

What a Comfort Thou Art

Like a fast-approaching storm moving over an unsuspecting lake,
Life's troubles, trials, and tribulations seem like more than I can take.
Depression encompasses me with a listlessness that makes me numb,
And I can't get up, function, call on dear friends, or eat more than a crumb.

I become a whining, self-centered shadow of my authentic self.
My sinking spirit shouts, "Helpless! Hopeless! Unlovable!" to myself.
If this overwhelmingly sick slide into self-pity lasts too long,
Crablike I withdraw, lost and alone, convinced that all I do is wrong.

It's in moments of deepest despair, I find God's gentle, tender care.
The Lord's love surrounds, enfolds, comforts, and encourages me to dare
To venture out among the living with the words, *Your faith has healed you.*
Go in peace, ringing in my ears as gratitude creeps back into view.

With God's grace and my salvation in Jesus—faith, hope, and love abound.
A peaceful calm, that replaces waves of inner suffering, is found.
"God's way is perfect!" my soul seems to sense with a flutter in my heart.
Like a strong, supportive hand on my shoulder, what a comfort Thou art!

Trust Completely

I depend on you and trusted you since I was young. – Psalm 71:5 (CEV)

The King was overjoyed and gave orders to lift Daniel out of the lion's den. And when Daniel was lifted from the den, no wound was found on him, because he had trusted in his God. – Daniel 6:23

Unharmed

Lord, lift me
Out of the lion's den.
Despite angry clawing
And savage slander,
Let me step out of this quagmire
With my eyes fully on you.
Unharmed,
Unwounded,
Unscarred,
Unscathed.
Then I will shout with joy
like Jeremiah who called the Lord
"My strength and my fortress,
My refuge in time of distress."*

I am reminded
That I have depended on you
And *trusted you*
Since I was young.
You have always been there
For me, Lord.
What you think of me matters most,
Not comments from meanspirited people.
They are not able to separate me
From your consistent
Unconditional love.
You let me know when I am in the wrong
And lift me up when I am right.
I depend on you.

---

* Jeremiah 16:19

Seek, Wait, Trust

Fear of man will prove a snare, but whoever trusts in the Lord is kept safe. – Proverbs 29:25

Help at Hand

There will be times you are filled
with panicky fear and dread,
acting irrationally—
even wishing you were dead.

Things may seem downright hopeless.
Discern the Lord's help at hand,
calling you from confusion,
despair and sin's stubborn stand.

At each crucial turning point
in your long-suffering life,
God's been there to rescue you
from every kind of strife.

The fear of man is a snare
which is full of distortions.
Don't get trapped by others' tricks.
Learn to trust the Lord's portions.

Put your hope fully in God
every hour, every day.
With his help, you'll face
each new trial along the way.

So always begin again;
that's why God made night and day.
No matter how bleak times seem,
growth happens along the way.

Such serenity allows
your grateful spirit to sing,
"This challenge is not the end
but a brand-new beginning!"

In you our fathers put their trust; they trusted you and you delivered them. They cried to you and were saved; in you they trusted and were not disappointed. But I am a worm and not a man, scorned by men and despised by people. All who see me mock me; they hurl insults, shaking their heads: "He trusts in the Lord; let the Lord rescue him, since he delights in him." Yet you brought me out of the womb; you made me trust in you even at my mother's breast. From birth I was cast upon you; from my mother's womb you have been my God. Do not be far from me, for trouble is near and there is no one to help. Those who seek the Lord will praise him. – Psalm 22:4-11, 26b

When Trouble Is Near

When trouble is near
and I feel helpless,
I can always count on my God
whom I have known from birth.
I delight in him,
not only because
he has delivered me in the past,
but also because he is able to rescue me
right here,
right now,
when I need him most.

Although I've been mocked
and insulted,
sworn at and scorned,
I don't have to let
those arrows—
intended to stab
my heart—
poison my spirit.
My strength
and self-worth
come from my savior.

I cry to you, O Lord.
You alone
will save me
from the sting of savage attacks.
*Do not be far from me,
for trouble is near
and there is no one to help*
apart from you.
Save me from all harm.
With praise I seek you,
and I trust in your deliverance.

"I will save you; you will not fall by the sword but will escape with your life because you trusted in me," declares the Lord. – Jeremiah 39: 18

Precarious

Decades ago, on a dark December evening,
an agitated, disheveled man
used his large, heavy duffle bag
to force his way into my house.
He tied me up and beat me for hours.
I could see in his detached eyes
he intended to kill me.
Wounded in body and mind,
but not in spirit,
I felt totally defenseless.
I called on the only help
I had at my disposal.
I silently prayed to the Lord.
I asked for immediate deliverance.
I begged God for the sake of my children,
asleep in the adjoining rooms,
to help me figure out a plan of escape.

The ropes on my wrist
were too tight to be loosened;
the knife at my throat too precarious to ignore.
Only calm could counter and diffuse
my attacker's deranged state.
"The Lord is my rock and my salvation.
Whom shall I fear?"*
I placed my trust in the Lord,
and God gave me the right words to say
so that the bonds were temporarily loosened.
Once released,
instead of going to the bathroom as I had feigned,
I tiptoed down two flights of stairs
and fled into the dark of the night.
Naked and wounded,
but no longer frightened,
I followed the Lord's path.

---

*   Psalm 27:1a

Grabbing a towel from the clothesline
to cover myself,
I crossed the street
in the dead of night
to knock on a friend's door.
We called the police.
They escorted my tormenter out
in handcuffs
and rescued my children.
Once they were safely asleep at her home,
an officer took me back to the scene.
The duffle bag, knife, and several guns
were strewn all over my bed.
One of the guns,
an antique rifle
with a bayonet attached,
made me shudder.

After all these years,
my pulse still quickens
as I read these words of scripture:
"I will save you;
you will not fall by the sword
but will escape with your life
because you trusted in me,"
declares the Lord.
That fateful night causes me to echo
the words of a favorite old hymn:
"O Joy that seekest me through pain,
I cannot close my heart to Thee;
I trace the rainbow through the rain,
and feel the promise is not vain,
that morn shall tearless be."[7]

Seek, Wait, Trust

You keep in perfect peace those whose minds are steadfast because they trust in you. Trust in the Lord forever, for the Lord, the Lord himself, is the Rock eternal. Yes, Lord, walking in the way of your laws, we wait for you: your name and renown are the desire of our hearts. – Isaiah 26:3-4, 8

Defining Moments

God will help you
Weather the storms of life,
Smoothing out
The rough edges,
Shaping rock-hard resilience,
If you trust in him.

Has the Lord ever rescued you
From death's door?
From a near-fatal accident?
Domestic violence?
Serious illness?
A natural disaster?

Defining moments
When you humbly see
Life can be snuffed out
As quickly as a candle
Or senselessly
By a stray bullet.

Such experiences
Make you grateful to be alive.
With *perfect peace* and surety,
You sense the Lord
Still has something special
Waiting for you.

You're willing to serve
In whatever way he wills.
After all, that's the least
And the best
You can do
For your *Rock eternal*.

Do not put your trust in princes, in mortal men, who cannot save. When their spirit departs, they return to the ground; on that very day their plans come to nothing. Blessed is he whose help is in the Lord his God, the maker of heaven and earth, the sea, and everything in them—the Lord, who remains faithful forever. He upholds the cause of the oppressed and gives food to the hungry. The Lord sets prisoners free, the Lord gives sight to the blind, the Lord lifts up those who are bowed down, the Lord loves the righteous. The Lord watches over the calm and sustains the fatherless and the widow. – Psalm 146:3-9a

Stay Close

You put your faith in me,
And I have been a disappointment
To you.
I tried to love you
As best I could,
But you always wanted more or less,
Or different,
Or difficult.

I am mortal;
I make mistakes.
I fall short.
I live and breathe
And die a little every day.
Only God,
Our creator,
Remains faithful forever.

Your heavenly Father will hold you up,
Feed you
And free you
From the things
That imprison you.
He'll give you a new vision
Of yourself
And of others.

The Lord will lift you out
Of the disappointments
That drag you down.
Stay close to him.
Seek his right way.
Wait patiently for his peaceful resolve,
Trusting in his protection
As he makes all things right.

Seek, Wait, Trust

I trust in you, Lord, and you will do something. – Psalm 38:15 (CEV)

Then he got into the boat and his disciples followed him. Without warning, a furious storm came up on the lake, so that the waves swept into the boat. But Jesus was sleeping. The disciples went and woke him, saying, "Lord, save us! We're going to drown!" He replied, "You of little faith, why are you so afraid?" Then he got up and rebuked the winds & the waves and it was completely calm. The men were amazed and asked, "What kind of man is this? Even the winds and the waves obey him!" – Matthew 8: 23-27

Inner Calm

There are people in life we fear.
Every encounter with them
is as shaky as a small boat
tossed about in deep water
during a windstorm.
Their battering disdain
throws us
into a sea of despair.

Disrespected,
shut out,
without common ground,
we find ourselves adrift,
lost and alone,
overwhelmed by their stormy temperaments.
In such chaotic confusion,
our energy swirls around them.

Remembering Jesus
is the one who stills the water
reminds us to place our trust in him.
An inner calm spreads over us.
Unconditional love awaits us
as we redirect our course;
with God as our focal point,
the way becomes clear.

Trust Completely

Submitting our will to his,
we find not only a safe refuge
but also a changed attitude.
Our fear has been replaced
with courage and newfound patience.
We discover other people
don't throw us off course;
we do that to ourselves.

God doesn't send our problems;
he gives us Jesus to meet challenges.
When we're willing to follow him,
he becomes the captain
of all our future journeys.
We are amazed at his ability to help us
weather bad times as well as good
with tranquility.

Seek, Wait, Trust

Praise the Lord. Blessed are those who fear the Lord, who find great delight in his commands. They will have no fear of bad news; their hearts are steadfast, trusting in the Lord. Their hearts are secure, they will have no fear, in the end they will look in triumph on their foes. – Psalm 112:1, 7-8

Calming Protection

I need your guidance, Lord.
    Please direct my path
        so my heart remains *steadfast*
            and courage replaces my fears.

Save me from the snares
    and land mines of mean-spirited malice.
        With your help and guidance,
            I will lovingly *triumph* over those who put me down.

Knowing you right all wrongs,
    I rest in the knowledge
        that you will securely protect me
            and keep me from harm's way.

I *delight* in your instructions
    and *have no fear of bad news*.
        Like an indestructible shield,
            the shelter of your arms ensures my safety.

I am not asking you, Lord,
    to punish or avenge anyone.
        Jesus taught us to love our enemies;
            I humbly ask you to soften their hearts and mine.

As I place my trust in you, Lord,
    bless me with your grace-filled love
        and the calming protection
            only your patient peace provides.

Trust in the Lord and do good; dwell in the land and enjoy safe pasture. Delight yourself in the Lord and he will give you the desires of your heart. Commit your way to the Lord; trust in him and he will do this: He will make your righteousness shine like the dawn, the justice of your cause like the noonday sun. – Psalm 37:3-6

Heart's Desire

I am grateful I have lived long enough
    to witness the working out
        of some of your plans for me
            and my loved ones.

A lifetime of daily delighting in you,
    seeking your guidance and reading your Word,
        praising you and praying for your guidance
            has helped me trust in your faithfulness.

Over the years you have led me to safety and serenity.
    My trust is in you, O Lord.
        You have even given me my heart's desire—
            a loving partner with whom to grow old.

With the wisdom born of longevity,
    I commit myself to doing your will.
        Someday may my kindness *shine like the dawn*
            and my dedication to justice *like the noonday sun.*

Seek, Wait, Trust

Blessed is he who trusts in the Lord. – Proverbs 16:20b

God in Whom We Trust

Job may have lost
Everything,
But he never stopped
Trusting in the Lord.
In the end,
God blessed him
With family,
Friends,
Great wealth,
And a long life.

Even at the point of losing
Everything,
We must never stop
Trusting in you, Lord.
From generation to generation,
Believers are part of your beloved family.
You bless us each like a treasured guest,
Supplying all our needs as the perfect host,
Loving us
Throughout eternity.

Trust Completely

I obey you with all my heart, and I trust you, knowing that you will save me. – Psalm 25:21 (CEV)

In that day they will say, "Surely this is our God, we trusted in him, and he saved us. This is the Lord, we trusted in him; let us rejoice and be glad in his salvation." – Isaiah 25:9

On the Battlefield

Each minute of this cross-country flight
brings me closer to you, to your pain,
to your illness, to your vulnerability, to your mortality.
Pneumonia almost took you from me
like it ushered in the last few weeks of your brother's life.
I have said prayers hoping to out-pray my fears.
God would remove those fears
if I would truly let go and leave you in his loving care.

I feel a desperate need to remain vigilant...
after all, your brother died on my watch.
I have no power over the bacteria
cursing through your body.
I pray the doctors and medical scientists
find every strain that needs to be eradicated.
In like fashion, may God wipe out my fear
before I stand next to you in your hospital room.

I want to bring you strength not panic,
loving presence not isolation,
hope not dread, and faith born of trust not doubt.
I want to model LIFE and the courage it takes to fight to live
when you are on the battlefield.
Our merciful God has heard the collective prayers
of your family and loved ones asking that your life be spared.
Warrior Princess, your inner faith will help win the battles ahead.

I wish I could forge ahead of you on the front line
taking out all that threatens your well-being.
Instead, my only role is to hold your hand and whisper prayers
to our God whose love for you is far beyond our human understanding.
In immense pain, we often feel his presence the most.
Rest in his comforting arms,
but stay in this world for the sake of your children and your mother
who loves you far beyond the distance I've traveled tonight.

Seek, Wait, Trust

I trust in the Lord. I will be glad and rejoice in your love, for you saw my affliction and knew the anguish of my soul. – Psalm 31:6b

At Work

Like Atlas,
my heart is heavy
with the weight of the world.
My migraines are as real
as the mighty thunder
rolling across the sky.
A lightning bolt
reminds me
you have not deserted me.
You see my affliction and anguish.
Please lift my waning spirit
and grant me blessed rest.

You're at work
in everything, Lord.
Help me to never doubt that.
Life's rainbow-like moments
remind me
that you keep
your caring covenant
with each generation.
You restore
rather than destroy;
you forgive
rather than condemn.

You know what's best for me.
Let me find comfort in your love.
Help me feel your presence
at work in my life.
With your help,
pain can become
a pathway that leads
to deeper understanding
and an opportunity for growth.
I want to always say
with assurance,
I trust in the Lord.

And again, I will put my trust in him. – Hebrews 2:13

Your Amazing Grace

Lord, help me trust
your way
is perfect.
You are in control,
not me!
Forgive my arrogance,
my insensitivity
and my willfulness.
Replace fear
with your amazing grace
and perfect ways.
Please, make me whole.

Lord, help my family learn
letting go of the past
and trusting the future to you
bring joy now.
Childhood hurts—
once forgiven—
can be steppingstones
to inner healing and healthy interactions.
Replace fear
with your amazing grace
and perfect ways.
Please, make my family whole.

Lord, help humanity realize
there cannot be peace
while we're separated from each other
through hatred and prejudice.
Harmony reflects your diverse kingdom.
Fill us with the love
you demonstrated
while we were still sinners.
Replace fear
with your amazing grace
and perfect ways.
Please, make your people whole.

Seek, Wait, Trust

At one time we too were foolish, disobedient, deceived and enslaved by all kinds of passions and pleasures. We lived in malice and envy, being hated and hating one another. But when kindness and love of God our Savior appeared, he saved us, not because of righteous things we have done, but because of his mercy. He saved us through the washing of rebirth and renewal by the Holy Spirit who he poured out in us generously through Jesus Christ, so that, having been justified by his grace, we might become heirs having the hope of eternal life. This is a trustworthy saying. And I want to stress these things so that those who have trusted in God may be careful to devote themselves to doing what is good. – Titus 3:3-8a

Justified by His Grace

We have been *foolish*
And *disobedient*.
Passions and pleasures
Have *deceived and enslaved* us.
Our hearts have been filled
With hurtful thoughts and *envy*.
Despite our unworthiness,
Jesus, our savior,
Appears
With *kindness*,
Mercy,
And undying *love*.
Like a seasoned gardener
Tenderly caring
For a withered plant,
He washes away sin,
Renews our spirit,
And gives us new life
And purpose.
Justified by his grace,
We now *trust* God
More fully.
With renewed *hope*,
We *devote* our lives
To doing what is good
And joyfully flowering
Wherever he replants us.

They were helped in fighting them, and God delivered the Hagrites and all their allies over to them, because they cried out to him during the battle. He answered their prayers, because they trusted in him. – I Chronicles 5:20

Rock Solid

Like a smooth stone
Thrown with confidence
Over an accepting lake,
Sometimes
We skim past
A problem
Or challenge
Sighing with instant relief.
Other answers follow
Fervent prayer,
And belief is bolstered
By the ever faithful
Mountain-like
Grandeur of God.

When we trust in him,
Battles are won,
Enemies overcome,
Solutions found,
And hearts healed.
The Lord,
Who has remained
Rock solid
From generation
To generation,
Hears the cries
Of the weary
And the heartfelt prayers
Of the humble.

Seek, Wait, Trust

Let him who walks in the dark, who has no light, trust in the name of the Lord and rely on his God. – Isaiah 50:10b

God Bless You

For so long I have not known
How to pray for you
Other than to ask God to bless you.
Your needs and demands
Have overwhelmed me,
But nothing is impossible with God.

Today
Isaiah reminds me,
Although you may be walking
In darkness,
The Lord is always
Within a prayer's reach.

You may no longer call me,
But I pray you will trust in
And call on the name of the Lord.
Rely on God.
He, and he alone,
Will bring light into your darkness.

And when the Israelites saw the great power of the Lord displayed against the Egyptians, the people feared the Lord and put their trust in him and in his servant Moses. – Exodus 14:31

Trust in the Lord

When wheeled into surgery,
You place your physical well-being
In the hands of a respected surgeon
And trained medical support team.

If the aftermath of a life trauma
Threatens to thwart your future,
You seek the counsel
Of a mental health professional.

When your spiritual peace is shaky,
And life is weighing you down,
Put your trust in the Lord
Whose *great power* is on display always.

Seek, Wait, Trust

Hear, O Lord, and answer me, for I am poor and needy. Guard my life, for I am devoted to you. You are my God, save your servant who trusts in you. Have mercy on me, O Lord, for I call to you all day long. Bring joy to your servant, for to you, O Lord, I lift up my soul. – Psalm 86:1-4

Unexpected Moments

A tsunami of grief overtook me a few years ago
when I heartbreakingly discovered
your short nap had turned into eternal rest.
Primal screams mirrored the hurricane-force howl
of wind in my muddled mind.

The heaviest breakers,
that brought me to my knees in the early days
after your untimely death, have subsided.
The storm surge of tears has diminished in frequency
as an ebbtide wanes during a tidal phase.

But there are still unexpected moments
when a wave of sadness washes over me
like rising and falling rollers to a novice surfer.
Occasionally, I even need to grab something
nearby to catch my breath and my balance.

Most days now, mild depression
gently laps against the shoreline of my productive life.
Yet, keeping busy doesn't wipe away sadness
any more than a massive swell wipes away
all the debris it deposits on even the most pristine beach.

Today's sea sounds are meditatively serene as I stand
by the water's edge on this anniversary of your death.
Over time, calm has replaced fear; peace has overtaken panic.
Hope, like a groundswell, has restored laughter and levity,
and joy is beginning to outpace grief.

Sunbeams add a little heavenly warmth
to this appropriately chilly morning.
Marveling at each white-capped wave,
I thank God your life washed over mine
with a permanence that even death cannot erase.

Trust in him, at all times, O people; pour out your hearts to him, for God is our refuge. – Psalm 62:8

Our Refuge

O strong and loving God
You are our refuge in times of trouble,
Our joy in the depths of sorrow,
Our calm amidst chaos,
And the wisdom correcting our weaknesses.
Cleanse us of fear, doubt, and childish desires,
So we may sense your presence in our lives.

Teach us to truly trust you always:
From day's beginning
To evening's end,
Whether the day brings tears or laughter,
Shadows or sunshine,
Loss or gain,
Bereavement or blessings.

For when we pour our hearts out to you,
Our spirits seem more serene,
Our faith feels firmer,
And our hope is eternal.
Hold us in the hallow of your hand
Until we have been strengthened
By your unfailing love.

Seek, Wait, Trust

Sovereign Lord, you are God! Your covenant is trustworthy, and you have promised these good things to your servant. – II Samuel 7:28

The Promise Fulfilled

A human promise
once verbalized
with the intent
to follow through
is hopefully realized,
sometimes delayed,
or occasionally broken.

I can confidently
bring all my concerns before you,
Sovereign Lord.
You are God!
I know you are *trustworthy*
as I whisper
my lifelong love for you.

You deserve all praise,
gracious God,
for the vows
you have made
and kept.
Generations have benefited
from your faithfulness.

Throughout history,
your divine promises,
have always been
perfectly realized,
sometimes delayed
to the appropriate moment,
but never broken,

Your grace is amazing.
I can say with assurance
that you have kept
your centuries-long covenant;
your Son Jesus,
my Lord and Savior,
is your ultimate promise fulfilled.

But I am like an olive tree flourishing in the house of the Lord; I trust in God's unfailing love forever and ever. – Psalm 52:8

Imagine

Imagine
all the sunrises and sunsets
an olive tree witnessed
over the hundreds of years
that it flourished:
the storms it weathered,
the breezes it enjoyed,
the pruning it endured,
the patience
it displayed.

See
how Jesus reflected
his trust in God.
Planted through the Holy Spirit,
rooted in the Holy Word,
pruned with pain and sorrow,
watered with compassion and humility,
harvested for the sins of the world.
He is the vine;
we are the branches.

Produce
the fruit of *God's unfailing love*:
plant seed-like faith;
spread kindness and joy;
water fertile ground;
prune out indifference and hatred;
grow in the sunshine of grace;
and cultivate caring communities
where all flourish
as God truly intended.

Seek, Wait, Trust

Train a child in the way he should go, and when he is old he will turn to it. Pay attention and listen to the sayings of the wise; apply your heart to what I teach, for it is pleasing when you keep them in your heart and have them ready on your lips. So that your trust may be in the Lord, I teach you today, even you. – Proverbs 22:6, 17-19

Awestruck

I have tried my own way;
I uncovered a stubbornness
I still have not fully stamped out.
I have tried the world's way;
But its cold callousness
Constantly trips me up.

I have sought the Lord's way.
Through prayer
I have discovered roots
That were planted in me
When I was a child
Who trusted easily.

When I humble myself,
God shows the way,
Whispering wisdom
To my willing spirit.
I respond with awestruck,
Child-like faith.

But I trust in your unfailing love; my heart rejoices in your salvation. – Psalm 13:5

Save Me from Myself

Lord, save me from myself.
Dig out my faults and weaknesses
That sometimes
Turn into full-fledged
Errors and sins,
Stunting my growth
As a child of God.

Rooted in your word, plant the seeds
Of righteousness deep within me.
Cover me with grace
So that the temptations of life
Stop choking my growth like weeds.
Fertilize my fragile heart
With your faithful nurturing.

Cleanse my thoughts
And shape my deeds.
Prune away
Any tendency toward wrongdoing,
Selfishness,
Stubbornness,
And arrogance.

Provide the empowering sunlight
That comes only from your Son
And the encouragement
That comes only from your Spirit.
As my heart
Rejoices in your salvation,
Allow me to blossom abundantly.

Trusting in your *unfailing love*,
May my life
Bear plentiful fruit
Providing a healthy harvest
Of peace
And genuine care
For all my neighbors.

Seek, Wait, Trust

As the Scripture says, "Anyone who trusts in him will never be put to shame – the same Lord is Lord of all, and really blesses all who call on him." – Romans 10:11-12

Focus

You can't force others to show you respect,
But you can remove yourself
From the shame and blame dance
Often jointly choreographed.

To refrain from dysfunctionality,
Learn to "detach with love" from the cruel
Person permeating your thoughts.
Focus instead on God.

Anyone who trusts in him
Will never be put to shame.
With a humble heart seek full forgiveness
For mistakes made and sins spawned.

Lean on the Lord;
The *Lord of all really blesses all who call on him.*
God sees the sacrifices you've made for others
And feels your honest, heartfelt faith.

He has provided all your needs
In the toughest of times.
He will protect you still;
Put your trust in God.

I will instruct you and teach you in the way you should go; I will counsel you with my loving eye on you. Do not be like the horse or the mule, which have no understanding but must be controlled by bit and bridle or they will not come to you. Many are the woes of the wicked, but the Lord's unfailing love surrounds the one who trusts in him. – Psalm 32:8-10

Simple Trust

It has become apparent
to all who continue to love you
that the worldly woes
which surround you
directly result
from the caustic ways
you interact with others.

Come back
to the simple trust
you had for God in your childhood.
He *will counsel you.*
He still has his *loving eye on you.*
The Lord's unfailing love
surrounds the one who trusts in him.

Do not be as stubborn as a mule;
turn your life over to God's tender care.
The Lord *will instruct you*
and teach you in the way you should go.
When you're able to love God fully,
you'll be able to love yourself again.
Then, finally, you'll be able to love others.

Seek, Wait, Trust

He who dwells in the shelter of the Most High will rest in the shadow of the Almighty. I will say of the Lord, "He is my refuge and my fortress, my God, in whom I trust." – Psalm 91:1-2

Shadows

I remember, as a child,
Walking next to my father.
Spotting our shadows on the sidewalk,
I would skip ahead trying to make my little shadow
Reach as tall as his.

That was impossible.
But, when I stepped to the side,
I discovered
My shadow could disappear inside his.
That made me giggle with delight.

I still need to *rest in the shadow of the Almighty.*
The world is weighing me down, Lord.
I need to disappear for awhile
In the comfort and security of your love.
In the shelter of your all-powerful wings, I find refuge.

There I can breathe in your goodness
And exhale the negativity
That has overwhelmed my usually happy spirit.
In the safety of your fortress, I can focus on your will
And your way until I get my bearings again.

Then, refreshed and renewed
By *my God, in whom I trust,*
I will be able to return
To life's many challenges
With joy and gratitude.

After daily walking with you, Lord,
The next time I spot my shadow
I will have my head erect,
Shoulders back,
And a skip in my step.

He who was seated on the throne said, "I am making everything new." Then he said, "Write this down for these words are trustworthy and true." He said to me: "It is done. I am the Alpha and Omega, the Beginning and the End. To him who is thirsty, I will give to drink without cost from the spring of the water of life." – Revelations 21:5-6

I Thirst

I am thirsty for righteousness
and the knowledge of your will for me.
I am thirsty for your deep presence in my life, Lord,
and for "the peace that passes all understanding."*
I am thirsty for wholeness
and the ability to love others as you have loved me.
I am thirsty for acceptance
and the mercy only you can provide.
I am thirsty for justice
and a world that reflects your kingdom on earth.

I thirst for your wisdom
streaming from your Holy Word.
I thirst for a life of meaning
surging with the passion of Christ.
I thirst for the new wine
flooding from your fountain of forgiveness.
I thirst for life eternal
gushing with the faith that leads to life.
I thirst for redemption
flowing from the blood of Jesus.

I've learned
my thirst is only quenched by
the spring of the water of life
from which your beloved son Jesus,
the Alpha and Omega,
makes everything, including me, new.
With humility and gratitude
for the cup of salvation he supplies,
may I become an overflowing
vessel of love.

---

* Philippians 4:7

Seek, Wait, Trust

We will tell the next generation the praiseworthy deeds of the Lord, his power and the wonders he has done. He decreed statutes for Jacob and established his law in Israel, when he commanded our forefathers to teach their children, so the next generation would know them, even the children yet to be born, and they in turn could tell their children. Then they would put their trust in God and would not forget his deeds but would keep his commands. – Psalm 78:46-47

Throughout History

Sociologists call this
the post-Christian era,
but those of us who still believe
have an obligation to pass faith on
to *the next generation.*
We must demonstrate
to young people
the praiseworthy deeds of the Lord.
His power and great wonders
have awed believers
throughout history.

Our creator commands
that we teach
his laws and statutes
to our children,
and they in turn
could tell their children.
Then they would put their trust in God.
All God's children
are our children;
all need
a faith foundation.

Let's give them solid roots,
grounded in the knowledge
that the Lord's miraculous power
still protects and saves.
Our children will only believe
if our faith is real…
not just in words but also in actions.
In order for them to blossom today
and bear fruit tomorrow,
we must be abundant branches
in Christ's vineyard.

Some trust in chariots and some in horses, but we trust in the name of the Lord. – Psalm 20:7

A Matter of Trust

Some admire fancy cars and status symbols;
others put their faith in stocks and bonds.
Many obtain worldly knowledge,
while countless folks follow charismatic leaders.
This group believes in nature;
that group thinks nurture has the greater impact.
Plenty of people prize the comfort of their own home,
while fewer value the freedom of the open road.
Lots revere the most recent rock star;
even more idolize their winning sports team.
Some individuals value their profession;
others prize their favorite pastime.
Most couples adore their children,
while others cherish their pets.

But we trust in the name of the Lord.
As children of God,
we believe
he accepts us,
protects us,
supports us,
rewards us,
guides us,
saves us,
and loves us.
He helps us to stand tall,
and he answers us
when we call
on his holy name.

Seek, Wait, Trust

My people, you are my witnesses and my chosen servant. I want you to know me, to trust me, and understand that I alone am God. I have always been God; there can be no others. – Isaiah 43:10 (CEV)

But the Lord said to Moses and Aaron, "Because you did not trust in me enough to honor me as holy in the sight of the Israelite, you will not bring this community into the land I give them." – Numbers 20:12

There Are Consequences

Moses and Aaron learned
There are consequences for not trusting God.
They could lead the way,
But they would not reach their new home.
They could wander in the wilderness
For forty years,
But they would never arrive.
With compassion,
The Lord showed them
A mountaintop view of the Promised Land
Their people would inherit.

Dr. Martin Luther King, Jr.
Saw the Promised Land, too,
The night before he died.
He said he had been to the mountaintop.
God tells all who are willing to listen:
My people, you are my witnesses
And my chosen servant.
I want you to know me, trust me,
And understand that I alone am God.
I have always been God.
There can be no others!

The cost of not trusting the Lord
Is more than you can bear,
So as you give your problems
Over to God,
Don't snatch them back again.
Remember he always
Has your best interest in mind.
God Almighty
Has the power
To change your life for the better
If you trust and follow where he leads.

The one who trusts will never be dismayed. I will make justice the measuring line and righteousness the plumb line. – Isaiah 28:16b-17a

The Plumb Line

God expects all his children to be reconcilers
Whenever we see brokenness.
We, too, are broken as long as we're separated
From people we assume are least like us.

In today's angry polarized world,
God challenges us to see *righteousness* as his plumb line
For measuring how we love our neighbors.
Just appreciating differences isn't enough.

Love requires spending time together,
Listening with an open heart and speaking with sensitivity,
Sharing common dreams and goals,
And seeking truth with the measuring line of justice.

Steeples are strongest when the force of gravity is evenly dispersed.
So, too, the Lord created us humans to be most stalwart
When the lines that arbitrarily separate us
Are erased with intentional inclusivity.

Accepting others with newfound respect,
Sharing feelings and perceptions,
Taking risks and earning trust
Build friendship and promote peace.

Without the use of a plumb line,
Walls that are not vertical
Eventually deform and can even collapse
Whole buildings.

Walls of hatred, fear, and indifference
Must be broken down wherever we encounter them
Before they destroy God's beloved creation—
Even when that means facing our own brokenness.

*O house of Israel, trust in the Lord – he is their help and shield.
O house of Aaron, trust in the Lord – he is their help and shield.
You who fear him, trust in the Lord – he is their help and shield.
The Lord remembers us and will bless us. He will bless
the house of Israel, he will bless the house of Aaron, he will bless
those who fear the Lord – small and great alike.* – Psalm 115:9-13

How Blessed I Am

My father has always been a blessing in my life
and in the lives of countless others.
At ninety-seven,
his strength, wit, and intelligence
have not faltered.
He is the reason
David's description of God
resonates with me.
My dad has helped me with everything
from skinned knees to a bruised ego.
He's removed splinters,
loose teeth,
and even my ex-husband
who had refused to leave
after the divorce was final.

Over the years,
Dad's protective arms
have shielded me
from physical
and emotional disasters.
That's not to say
he didn't allow me
to experience
and grow from
my fair share
of hard knocks.
He did.
Yet he was always there
with wisdom and comfort
when I needed it most.

Trust Completely

My greatest fear
was disappointing my dad,
and I never wanted to make him mad.
My father forgives easily,
but he forgets nothing.
He is comfortable in all settings,
because he's comfortable with himself.
Although he's a man's man,
he's also a pied piper with children.
Women, too, are attracted
to his ruggedly handsome looks
and laid-back charm,
but for seventy years, before her death,
he only had eyes for my mother,
the love of his life.

If my earthly father is only a dim reflection
of my heavenly Father,
then undoubtedly,
God is a God in whom I can always trust.
He is my help and shield.
He never falters or fails to meet me
at the point of my deepest need.
He encourages with His presence,
remembers with hope,
protects with His grace,
forgives with mercy,
strengthens with His power,
blesses with compassion,
and provides with His love.
How blessed I am to be a child of God!

Seek, Wait, Trust

Idols can't send rain, and showers don't fall by themselves. Only you control the rain so we can put our trust in you the Lord our God. – Jeremiah 14:22 (CEV)

This is what the Lord says, "Cursed is the man who trusts in man, who depends on flesh for his strength and whose heart turns away from the Lord. He will be like a bush in the wasteland, he will not see prosperity when it comes. He will dwell in the parched places of the desert, in the saltland where no one lives. But blessed is the man who trusts in the Lord, whose confidence is in him. He will be like a tree planted by the water that sends out its roots by the stream. It does not fear when heat comes; its leaves are always green. It has no worries in a year of drought and never fails to bear fruit. – Jeremiah 17:5-8

No Need to Fear

The Lord compares trusting in man
and turning away from God
to a parched bush
in the desert,
while trusting in God
is like a well-nurtured tree
planted by a stream.
No matter how hot it gets,
the latter's leaves are always green.

People who put their trust in human idols
end up deserted.
In contrast,
those who trust in the Lord
need not fear.
When trouble comes,
they will still be nourished.
So blessed, they will continue to blossom
and *bear fruit.*

Jeremiah also reminds us,
Idols can't send rain,
and showers don't fall
by themselves.
Only the Lord controls the rain.
We would be wise
to follow the prophet's timeless wisdom
and *put our trust*
in the Lord our God.

See, I lay a stone in Zion, a chosen and precious cornerstone, and the one who trusts in him will never be put to shame." – I Peter 2:6

So this is what the Sovereign Lord *says: "See, I lay a stone in Zion, a tested stone, a precious cornerstone for a sure foundation; the one who relies on it will never be stricken with panic. –* Isaiah 28:16

Just as God says in the Scriptures, "Look! I am placing in Zion a stone to make people stumble and fall. But those who have faith in that one will never be disappointed."– Romans 9:33 (CEV)

The One Who Trusts

Amidst the steady
storms of life,
she stands firm in faith,
seeking solace in her Savior,
waiting with inner calm.
Christ is her *precious cornerstone*.
The one who trusts in him
will never be put to shame.

Beyond bountiful blessings
or everyday disappointments,
he remains devoted to God,
seeking deeper meaning,
waiting for spiritual guidance.
He has rested on *a sure foundation*.
The one who relies on it
will never be stricken with panic.

Through joys, sickness, and struggles,
they place their trust in the Lord,
seeking serenity in all situations,
waiting for a sign or a miracle.
Jesus is the keystone of their confidence.
God says in the Scriptures…
those who have faith in that one
will never be disappointed.

Seek, Wait, Trust

But as for me, I trust in you. – Psalm 55:23b

I Trust in You

Lovers leave,
Friends betray confidences,
Family members move away,
Co-workers talk behind our backs,
Partners lash out in anger,
Children demand more than we can give,
Neighbors ignore our needs,
Acquaintances disappoint,
But as for me,
I trust in you,
O Lord.

You are faithful,
Unfailing,
Ever-present,
Loyal,
Calm and protective,
Giving,
Comforting
And steadfast.
But as for me,
I trust in you,
O Lord.

Let the morning bring me word of your unfailing love, for I have put my trust in you. Show me the way I should go, for to you I entrust my life. – Psalm 143:8

Emergence

Life becomes as welcoming as a warm spring day
When pre-morning devotions allow the release
Of fears, replacing all my doubts with profound peace.
I trust in *your unfailing love* to show the way.

I trade my earthly troubles for undeserved grace
And am willing to follow with wide open eyes.
As newfound serenity paints a calm sunrise,
The sun sparkles off the renewal taking place.

I thankfully emerge from my cave-like cocoon,
Flying through feats I was once unable to try.
Like a beautiful multi-colored butterfly,
My sacred wings flutter to your unending tune.

Seek, Wait, Trust

And Barnabus appointed elders for them in each church and with prayer and fasting, committed them to the Lord, in whom they had put their trust. – Acts 14:23

Streams of Light

As the communion meal is prepared,
Active and former *appointed elders*,
Both members and visitors, are called forward
Forming a circle beneath the cathedral's dome.
We are served the bread and wine together
In Edinburgh's ancient twelfth century edifice,
While the choir sings an ageless hymn
As old as the church.

I shed tears of joy in the very spot
Where saints of old once stood.
St. Giles Cathedral is cold, dark, and damp
Except for streams of light from above,
Like flames of fire warming weathered souls.
Infused with the Holy Spirit,
Trusting in an ever-present God,
My heart hums in sweet solidarity:

"Jesus, the very thought of you
Fills us with sweet delight
But sweeter far your face to view
And rest within your light.
No voice can sing, no heart can frame,
Nor can the mind recall
A sweeter sound than your blest name,
O Savior of us all.

O hope of ev'ry contrite soul,
O Joy of all the meek,
How kind you are to those who fall!
How good to those who seek!
O Jesus, be our joy today;
Help us to prize your love;
Grant us at last to hear you say:
Come, share my home above."[8]

All this is from God, who reconciled us to himself through Christ and gave us the ministry of reconciliation: that God was reconciling the world to himself in Christ, not counting people's sins against them. And he has committed to us the message of reconciliation. We are therefore Christ's ambassadors, as though God were making his appeal through us. We implore you on Christ's behalf: Be reconciled to God. God made him who had no sin to be sin for us, so that in him we might become the righteousness of God. – II Corinthians 5:18-21

The Firm Foundation

Honestly facing our own shortcomings shows us
Which actions and attitudes we ought to adjust.
Turning to him overcomes those flaws.
Isn't that why in God we must trust?

Nothing is ever solved by hiding from the truth
Or justifying our misguided behavior
Fueled by our faults and self-deceptions.
Isn't that why we need a savior?

Our Lord's reconciling, unconditional love
Is the firm foundation and hope on which we build
A fresh faith-based grateful lease on life.
Isn't that why we are spirit-filled?

He guides us, holds us, and picks us up when we fall.
Leaning on his Holy Word helps us discover
His salvation is able to turn our troubles around.
Isn't that how our lives recover?

Seek, Wait, Trust

Leave the orphans, I will protect their lives. Your widows too can trust in me. – Jeremiah 49:11

Protected

If you protect orphans and widows,
    surely I can trust
        my family
            to you, O Lord,
                for safekeeping.

Shelter them
    from the world's evils:
        self-centered arrogance,
            drugs and violence,
                and hard-hearted hatred.

Free them
    from financial snares,
        commercial glitz and greed,
            and the many mindless diversions
                that make up modern times.

Place a band
    of angels around them
        so the paths they each take
            are not only protected
                but also providentially planned.

Help me to always remember
    they are your children
        for eternity
            on loan to me
                for but a fleeting moment.

But be very careful to keep the commandment and the law that Moses the servant of the Lord gave you: to love the Lord your God, to walk in all his ways, to obey his commands, to hold fast to him and to serve him with all your heart and all your soul. – Joshua 21:5

Valuable Lessons

Having sometimes lost
    at love while subconsciously
        excusing myself of all blame,
            I must turn to the Lord
                humbly,
                      honestly,
                            wholeheartedly.

Having usually failed
    to realize the damage I was doing to others
        through my enabling and controlling actions,
            I must consider my role
                carefully,
                      conscientiously,
                            courageously.

Having occasionally wanted
    to give up and never love again
        to avoid the risk of yet another rejection,
            I must seek God's guiding spirit
                readily,
                      responsively,
                          reflectively.

Having ultimately learned
    the most valuable life lessons
        from the repeated mistakes I have made,
            I must *walk in all his ways*
                sincerely,
                      soulfully,
                          steadfastly.

Having finally grown
    past the pain and fear to rise above it
        while fully embracing today and tomorrow,
            I must reclaim the lovable parts of myself…
                tender,
                      thoughtful,
                          trusting.

Seek, Wait, Trust

Hezekiah trusted in the Lord, the God of Israel. There was no one like him among all the kings of Judah, either before or after him. But, they would not listen and were as stiff-necked as their fathers, who did not trust the Lord. He held fast to the Lord and did not cease to follow him; he kept the commands the Lord had given Moses. And the Lord was with him; he was successful in whatever he undertook. – II Kings 18:5-7a

Our Very Best

We all long to be the best at something:
gymnasts strive for a flawless 10;
bowlers a 300 game;
an ace for a tennis player;
a hole-in-one for a golfer.
Artists crave unflawed color
and composition.
Some students achieve
a perfect SAT or ACT score;
others at an early age
are child prodigies.

In his own time,
Hezekiah was considered
the best king to ever rule Israel.
To what did he attribute his success?

He *trusted in the Lord*,
like the athlete, student,
or concert violinist
who bow their heads
or point their finger heavenwards
in reverence
and in awe.
Each is humbly aware that talent
is a gift from God.
God works
to perfect us.

We become our very best
when we trust
and follow God
above all others.

Trust Completely

Those who trust in the Lord are like Mount Zion, which cannot be shaken but endures forever.
— Psalm 125:1

An Unmovable Force

Like a mountain,
God is steadfast,
strong,
and magnificent.
His creative powers
outweigh
the finite forms of life
and vegetation
found on all the mountain ranges
of the earth combined.

As the God of history,
he is an unmovable force
who cannot be denied.
He is the same today,
yesterday and tomorrow.
His arms are so long
and his infinite love is so deep
that he can reach
from the highest mountain peak
to the lowest valley to meet our needs.

His awesome powers
are so far beyond our human
capacity to understand,
yet he treasures each of us
as if we, ourselves,
had mountain grandeur.
With such affirmation,
our faith *cannot be shaken*.
All things are made possible
when we *trust in the Lord*.

Seek, Wait, Trust

He put a new song in my mouth, a hymn of praise to our God. Many will see and fear and put their trust in the Lord. – Psalm 40:3

The Voice of an Angel

I took voice lessons
in high school.
Despite having a good voice,
I almost failed the course
because I was painfully shy.

The more my teacher
screamed at me to sing out,
the more inhibited I got
until my voice was barely
a whisper.

A classmate told the teacher,
"You should hear
her sing at church;
there—
she has the voice of an angel!"

It seems
my vocal cords
are stimulated
by praise,
not fear.

I may never be a soloist,
but I can joyfully shout
"Hallelujah!"
because the Lord
put a new song in my mouth.

It is *a hymn of praise to our God*
who promises that one day
I will join the chorus of believers who
put their trust in the Lord
and sing his praises forever.

Do not let your heart be troubled. Trust in God; trust also in me. In my Father's house are many rooms; if it were not so, I would have told you. I am going there to prepare a place for you. I will come back and take you with me that you also may be where I am. – John 14:1-3

A Room of Her Own

I still hear the enchanting lilt
of my mother's soprano voice
filling the memories of my childhood.
She grew up poor in a large family,
and at a young age, endured her mother's death.
Over the years, her heart could have been troubled or sad;
instead, it hummed with happiness.

She knew how to make sacrifices:
toiled for us without complaint,
returned her own gifts
to buy something special for each of us,
and worked the hospital's late-night shift
to devote her days to making our house
a reliable refuge for the neighborhood.

At bedtime she would sing a sweet lullaby,
"Inky dinky bob-o-linky,
dream awhile and then…
your mommy will be waiting here
when you wake up again."
Once she wiped away a tear and whispered,
"That was my mother's song; now it's yours."

She never had a place to call her own growing up,
but her singing spirit filled each room in our home.
The key to her serenity was found
in her favorite Bible verse:
In my Father's house are many rooms;
If it were not so,
I would have told you.

She always trusted in the Lord
and believed her final haven
would be a room of her own in heaven
that Jesus had already prepared for her.
I can picture her right now,
snuggling with her mother, sisters, & oldest grandson,
blending their serene voices with the celestial choir.

*Put your trust in the light while you have it,
so that you become sons and daughters of light.* – John 12:36

A Ray of Hope

Out of the void,
the first thing God created was light.
At the darkest points in history,
his prophets illumined the way.
God sent his own Son
to be the light of the world.
Over a small stable in Bethlehem,
a star shone so bright
it was seen a continent away,
enlightening the world
with his birth.

This world still weighs us down
unless we tap into
what lies deep within us…
"embers of primeval fire"[9]
where God,
our creator,
continues to forge a home
for us.
There,
in his presence,
our hearts are set aglow.

If we put our trust in that illumination,
we, too, *become sons
and daughters of light.*
We might only be a flicker
in comparison to him,
but a flicker of peace
in a world filled with fear
and violence
is a golden ray of hope
which spreads
the glow of God's grace.

Trust Completely

Such spirit-filled,
Christ-like love,
like a flashlight on a moonless night
or a candle during an electric storm,
sheds light on countless lives.
Together believers form a stream
of compassion and consciousness
that cuts through human pain
and indifference
like a searchlight
breaking through dense fog.

Seek, Wait, Trust

God can be trusted, and he chose you to be partners with his Son, our Lord Jesus Christ.
– I Corinthians 1:9 (CEV)

Thanks be to God for his gift that is too wonderful for words. – II Corinthians 9:15

A Pathway to Peace

God in his infinite wisdom
And perfect timing
Created a pathway to peace
And reconciliation for you and me,
Both *partners with his Son, our Lord Jesus Christ.*

It came unexpectedly,
Like a rare taste of spring in February.
The ice was thawed,
The sun shone,
And hearts softened.

The warmth of your voice,
The humility of your manner,
The trust you've placed in the Lord
Have added a maturity
And a sincerity that is palpable.

Having sought God actively during your absence,
Having waited for the playing out of his will,
I am grateful we each trusted in his goodness.
Thanks be to God for his gift
That is too wonderful for words.

May the God of hope fill you with all joy and peace as you trust in him so that you may overflow with hope by the power of the Holy Spirit. – Romans 15:13

His Healing Rays

Seeking God
Is like longing for a summer breeze
On a hot sultry afternoon.
If our focus is only on our momentary discomforts,
We might miss the solace
Our Advocate sends
To soothe our suffering soul.

Waiting for God,
Like anticipating rainfall during a draught,
May test our patience and perseverance.
God, in due time, provides the much-needed relief.
His love is "from everlasting to everlasting"*
So that (we) may overflow with hope
By the power of the Holy Spirit.

Trusting God
Allows us to joyfully experience
His peaceful presence.
We feel his healing rays
Wash over our heavy hearts,
Like a warm shower
Soothing a chilled body.

---

* Psalm 103:17

Seek, Wait, Trust

Oh Lord Almighty, blessed is the person who trusts in you. – Psalm 84:12

My Life Is Blessed

> My life is blessed;
> that's safe to say,
> because Christ rose
> on Easter Day.
> Because he lives,
> I do believe,
> eternal life
> I will receive.

My life is blessed; it's plain to see my precious Lord has called to me.
He bids me do his work on earth, and in return, he gives rebirth.
My life is blessed; I humbly see, because the Lord's forgiven me.
His sacrifice has set me free; I must forgive my enemies.

> My life is blessed;
> I now can see,
> for Jesus gave
> his life for me.
> Thus, shall I give
> to those in need
> and witness to
> the lambs I feed.
>
> My life is blessed;
> It's truth I say –
> Christ Jesus rose
> on Easter Day!
> I trust the love
> that I've received;
> I'll pass it on
> for I believe.

It is better to take refuge in the Lord than to trust in man. It is better to take refuge in the Lord than to trust in princes. The Lord is my strength and my song; he has become my salvation. – Psalm 118:8-9, 14

Come to Me, Child

As a child I would climb
into my father's lap for comfort
after being injured or scared
or rejected by a playmate.
Dad would say, "Come to me, child.
I will keep you safe."
I seek similar refuge
in my Heavenly Father
when I have failed or when I am afraid.

I feel God's unconditional love
drawing me as close
as a nursing child to her mother.
The Holy Spirit soothes me
like my mother's lullabies once did.
I am reminded that I am a beloved child.
When I am lonely
or disheartened,
I find solace in the Lord's loving arms.

Unlike many human parents,
God never disappoints.
I will always trust in the Lord
who provides safe shelter
and grants deliverance
even in the most troubling times.
The Lord is my strength
and my song;
he has become my salvation.

Seek, Wait, Trust

(Trust) the good news: what God promised our fathers,
he has fulfilled for us, their children, by raising up Jesus.
As it is written in the second Psalm: "You are my Son; today I have become your Father."
The fact that God raised him from the dead, never to decay, is stated in these words:
"I will give you the holy and sure blessing promised to David."
So it is stated elsewhere: "You will not let your Holy One see decay." – Acts 13: 32-35

Love in Full Bloom

Like weeds overtaking a flower bed,
dried-up incidents of intolerance
tried to destroy our Lord and Savior
Just as a stem can't support
the weight of a dying daffodil,
even the powers of Rome couldn't stop
the crucifixion of the root of Jesse.
God willed it,
and the people demanded it.
It was not a path others would have chosen,
but his willingness to trust his Father
allowed Jesus
to make the ultimate sacrifice
for humankind.

Neither the thorn that draws blood
nor each petal that drops
negate the memory
of the awe-inspiring beauty
of a perfect rose.
Death tried to rob Jesus
of his earthly mission.
He bore alone
the piercing pain of the nails,
the sword-stabbed side,
the blood-soaked crown of thorns,
the mockery and humiliation,
the loneliness and betrayal,
the debilitating thirst.

Trust Completely

Every day, since his resurrection,
proclaims his victory over death.
His ascension acclaims God's plan
to draw earth closer to heaven
and us closer to him.
His undying love lives forever.
Such redemptive power
reclaims wayward lives
with undeserved grace.
Jesus is perfect.
Like the Rose of Sharon,
he is pure and passionate,
caring and compassionate,
love in full bloom.

Seek, Wait, Trust

May your unfailing love come to me, O Lord, your salvation according to your promise; then I will answer anyone who taunts me, for I trust in your word. Never take your word of truth from my mouth, for I have put my hope in your laws. I will always obey your law, for ever and ever. I will walk about in freedom, for I have sought out your precepts. – Psalm 119:41-45

Soaring to New Heights

Like so many other trips to the sea,
My gaze into the ocean
Draws contemplative
Thoughts of your majesty
And my insignificance.
Your unfailing love
Is deeper and wider
Than the ocean's breadth and depth.
As my mystical musings
Take flight,
I reflect on the magnificence
Of your might.
I savor the Spirit's sweetness,
Soaring to new heights
Like the seagulls overhead.

As the waves address the jagged rocks
They crash up against,
May I gather enough momentum
From your teachings
To *answer anyone who taunts me*
When I am next faced with vain insults.
Like the surf lapping against the shoreline
Whose final destination
Has been pre-ordained,
I will walk about in freedom
According to your perfect plan…
Trusting in your promises,
Protected by your grace,
Guided by your goodness,
And strengthened in faith.

Trust Completely

You have persevered and have endured hardships for my name, and have not grown weary. Whoever has ears, let them hear what the Spirit says to the churches. To the one who is victorious, I will give the right to eat from the tree of life, which is in the paradise of God. – Revelations 2:3, 7

The Tree of Love

As if walking a wooden pirate's plank,
I was forced to jump into stormy waters
The day you, my beloved son, unexpectedly died.
Years later, I imagine
Its wood was from the Tree of Life
Which our Celtic ancestors saw
As a connection between life and death.
Pondering the most painful moment of my life,
I believe your unique energy
Continued on across space and time.

Energy is the first tenet of that tree and its equivalent,
The Tree of Knowledge of Good and Evil.
Adam and Eve ate its fruit longing to know everything.
You were always intrigued by things that fascinated you.
You seem to whisper to me now,
"Some say the tree of crucifixion was a descendant of that sacred tree;
Others surmise the cross was built from a nearby dogwood tree, a symbol of rebirth.
Don't grieve for me, mother, I have been given *the right to eat from the tree of life*.
Trust that God knows *you have persevered and have endured hardships*.
One day we will be together *in the paradise of God*."

Today on the anniversary of your death,
I find solace in a solitary oak tree we once observed together.
Laying flowers nearby in a heart-shaped pattern
Gratefully grants temporary peace to my grieving soul.
Its roots are in the soil, but its limbs reach for the sky
As my aching heart does when it longs to embrace you.
This tree of love, like the tree of life, breeds hope.
Each root anchors your memory to family and friends,
And its coppery-brown leaves embody the countless blessings
Your truncated life brought to me and all who loved you.

Seek, Wait, Trust

*Surely you have granted him unending blessings and made him glad
with the joy of your presence. For the king trusts in the Lord;
through the unfailing love of the Most High he will not be shaken.* – Psalm 21:6-7

*I have spoken to you of earthly things, and you did not believe;
how then will you believe if I speak of heavenly things?
The Son of Man must be lifted up, that everyone who believes in him
may have eternal life.* – John 3:12, 14b

Predestined

God knows our story
long before we're even born—
Jesus was a direct descendant of Judah
who sold his brother Joseph into slavery
to merchants selling myrrh…
myrrh,
a gift fit for a king,
brought to Jesus at his birth
by wise men bearing gifts.

For God knows our beginnings,
our struggles
and our pain,
as well as our story's end.
Jesus foretold his own death
to Nicodemus:
*The Son of Man must be lifted up,
that everyone who believes in him
may have eternal life.*

There
on the cross
Christ was again offered myrrh;
this time mixed with wine
to numb the pain.
But Jesus let the cup pass,
suffering, instead,
for our sake
and for our sins.

Trust Completely

Nicodemus must have known
nothing could ease the sting of death,
and yet he brought enough myrrh,
an oil made from the leaf of a rose
found in Africa,
for a royal burial.
At the borrowed tomb,
he tenderly bathed the wounded body
of his crucified Lord.

Our Savior's sacrificial death
was predestined.
God sent his son Jesus
to lift the human spirit
and procure an *unending blessing—eternal life*.
May we truly trust and serve the Lord
whose all-knowing, *unfailing love*
is the essential oil
that sooths all earthly anguish.

Seek, Wait, Trust

The Lord is good, a refuge in times of trouble. He cares for those who trust in him. – Nahum 1:7

In Times of Trouble

Oh Lord,
our creator,
the God of history,
the covenant-maker,
we praise you
as the source
of our strength.
We appreciate you
for being
our safe sanctuary.

We thank you
for your revelation
of love
exemplified in the gift
of your Son Jesus Christ
and the salvation he offers.
You care for us
in ways too deep
for our unworthy
human understanding.

Help us to live
in unbroken
unity with you,
putting our full trust
in your abundant love.
Strengthen us
when the lure
of the wayward world
tempts us to stray from you
and your teachings.

Give us a great hunger
for you
and for your righteousness.
Because of your grace,
goodness,
and guidance,
we can face uncertainty
with the confidence
that you will not leave
or forsake us.

Instead,
our hearts
are joined with yours
in prayer.
You dwell in us
through the Holy Spirit
in ever-increasing measures
as we deepen our love
for you
and for our neighbors.

May our hearts join
the chorus of believers
throughout the ages
who have sung out
with certainty:
The Lord is good,
a refuge
in times of trouble.
He cares
for those who trust in him.

Seek, Wait, Trust

> *(Seek and trust) God's love as you wait for the mercy of our Lord Jesus Christ to bring you to eternal life.* – Jude 1:21

Along the Journey of Faith*

We have sought you "willingly
and actively"*
all of our lives, Lord,
sometimes apathetically
we must confess,
but with impassioned intentionality
while writing this book.
As we bring it
to completion,
our hearts "gladly
and happily" rejoice.

You have been our help,
not only during the writing process,
but also throughout our lives.
As our shield
against worldly distractions,
disappointment
and dismay,
you have shown us
that you are the true source
of inner strength
and unconditional love.

We have waited "steadfastly...
with certainty of hope"
for you, O Lord.
Your Holy Word
and your comforting arms
have given us much needed rest.
We have tried not to grumble
in "foolish sadness"
or "empty sorrow"
nor to strive against you
in open defiance.

---

* Throughout this poem, words in quotation marks are from the Julian of Norwich quotation cited on page vii

Trust Completely

Instead,
we've learned
to "trust...completely"
in your will for us
and our loved ones.
Along this journey of faith,
you have "come suddenly"
in rainbow-like displays
of your presence
and "joyfully"
with the blessing of undeserved love.

Let us proclaim
your goodness,
for you alone
are worthy of our attention,
devotion,
and service.
We will continue
to keep your love alive,
seek your guidance always,
wait for the mercy of our Lord Jesus Christ,
and trust that you will *bring us to eternal life.*

Seek, Wait, Trust

The other spies said things that made our people afraid, but I completely trusted the Lord God. – Joshua 14: 8 (CEV)

This is how God showed his love among us: He sent his one and only Son into this world that we might live through him. This is love: not that we loved God, but that he loved us and sent his Son as an atoning sacrifice for our sins. Dear friends, since God so loved us, we ought to love one another. No one has ever seen God, but if we love one another, God lives in us and his love is made complete in us. – I John 4:9-12

Trust Completely

T*his is how God showed his love among us*: sending his son Jesus;

Removing our sins with Christ's *atoning sacrifice*; and promising eternal life.

Unearned grace is undeniably a gift from our understanding God.

S*ince God so loved us,*

Then *we ought to love one another.*

Continue to seek the Lord, *dear friends,*

Only God can make us whole:

Molding and reshaping us in his image;

Providing us with inner strength as we wait for the knowledge of his will for us;

Lifting our spirits when we are afraid, anxious, or alone.

Each time we help neighbors in need, comfort a child, or show sincere kindness,

Truly *God lives in us* as love.

Even though *no one has ever seen God,*

Let others see *his love is made complete in us…*

Yesterday, today, and tomorrow.

The Lord *is my shepherd, I lack nothing. He makes me lie down in green pastures, he leads me beside quiet waters, he refreshes my soul. He guides me along the right paths for his name's sake. Even though I walk through the darkest valley, I will fear no evil, for you are with me; your rod and your staff, they comfort me. You prepare a table before me in the presence of my enemies. You anoint my head with oil; my cup overflows. Surely your goodness and love will follow me all the days of my life, and I will dwell in the house of the* Lord *forever. – Psalm 23*

The Lord Provides

The Lord provides all our needs…
Whether that be rest when we're weary,
Hope when we're down,
Guidance when we stray,
Or courage in the face of death.
Be not afraid
For the God we **seek** is with us.

The Lord is our *shepherd*,
Loyally standing by us,
Comforting us,
Protecting us from our *enemies*.
We are honored guests at his party.
As we **wait** on the Lord,
His *goodness* surrounds us.

When we **trust** in the Lord,
We truly see the Lord provides:
Not just today,
Not just yesterday,
Not just in the near future,
Not just when it's easy—
But *forever.*

A TRUSTING PRAYER

Lord,

We pray that the power of heaven will majestically come with the Holy Spirit and bless one who calls out today in need of prayer. Father, you knew what she needed before she even asked for it. She's a daughter walking and stumbling and searching and seeking and yet holding on to your unchanging hands.

Lord, there are others right now who need you. Somebody just needs a word from heaven that everything is gonna be alright.* Many need to hear the voice of Jesus tenderly calling them to his throne. And, Lord, we pray that by his blood all matters of the heart and all conditions of the body, all ailments clouding people's sight and people's faith from being ever true to you, O God, will be improved through trust in you. We ask you, O Lord, to bring endurance to each soul waiting for your deliverance.

Somebody needs Jesus, the great healer to touch his bones, arthritically inclined; to open his eyes blurred with glaucoma allowing him new shades of seeing.

Heal hearts needing blood pumped through their arteries that life might be in them. Oh, somebody needs to be sanctified today by the blood of Jesus. Somebody needs to leave here today washed and Holy Spirit-filled.

Lord, send a messenger right now. Dispatch 10,000 angels that we might become ministers of healing and prophets of goodness; we might be gladiators against evil; and we might be like lambs walking with love.

Lord, there's so much suffering going on. There's somebody here today who hasn't even told a family member what she's going through. We pray right now that she'll just turn it over to you. We know you can make anything all right, because you're an awesome God.

There's no problem too big for God today! No worry too burdensome that God can't fix. Give it to God today. Give God your problems. Give God your

---

*   Al Green. "Everything Is Gonna Be Alright," *Soul Survivor* (Memphis: Ardent Studios, 1987), 1.

Trust Completely

worries. Give God your sickness. Give God your financial stresses. Give God your children problems. Give it to God right now and say, "With all power in heaven, God, you can make it right!"

Trust in God with all your heart this morning, with all your mind, and with all your soul, and with all your body. *Trust and obey for there's no other way** but to trust in Jesus, and everything will be all right. Alright? "Alright!"

If you serve a mighty God who makes everything all right say, *It's alright!* "It's alright!!!"

Can I get an Amen? "Amen!"

No Other Way

---

* Rev. J.H. Sammis, *Hymns New and Old* (NY: Fleming, H. Revell, 1887), 59.

ENDNOTES

Chapter 1

1. Sheila Upjohn, *All Shall Be Well: Revelations of Divine Love of Julian of Norwich* (London: Darton, Longman and Todd Limited, 1992), 16.

2. Howard Thurman, *Meditations of the Heart* (Boston: Beacon Press, 1953), 175-176.

3. Upjohn, 16.

4. Upjohn, 44.

Chapter 2

5. Gerard Manley Hopkins, "God's Grandeur," *The Poems of Gerard Manley Hopkins*, ed. by Robert Bridges (London: Humphrey Milford, 1918), 7.

Chapter 3

6. Upjohn, 44.

7. George Matheson, "O Love That Wilt Not Let Me Go," the last stanza of his 19th Century hymn.

8. Bernard of Clairvaux, "Jesus the Very Thought of You," attributed to St. Bernard in 1150, trans. by Edward Caswell in 1849.

9. George L. Mason, *Captive Cathay: An Historical Poem Narrating the Resistance of China to the Opium Trade and Her Sad Defeat, 1775-1860* (Shanghai: American Presbyterian Mission Press, 1893), 5.

BIBLIOGRAPHY

Hopkins, Gerard Manley. "God's Grandeur." *The Poems of Gerard Manley Hopkins*. Edited by Robert Bridges. London: Humphrey Milford, 1918.

"Jesus, the Very Thought of You." Attributed to Bernard of Clairvaux in 1150; translated by Edward Caswell in 1849. *Lutheran Book of Worship*. Minneapolis: Augsburg Publishing House, 1978.

Mason, George L. *Captive Cathay: An Historical Poem Narrating the Resistance of China to the Opium Trade and Her Sad Defeat, 1775-1860*. Shanghai: American Presbyterian Mission Press, 1893.

Matheson, George. "O Love That Will Not Let Me Go." *Lutheran Book of Worship*. Minneapolis: Augsburg Publishing House, 1978.

Thurman, Howard. *Meditations of the Heart*. Boston: Beacon Press, 1953.

Upjohn, Sheila. *All Shall Be Well: Revelations of Divine Love of Julian of Norwich*. London: Darton, Longman and Todd Limited, 1992.

INDEX OF POEMS

A Beacon of Hope, 37
A Close Encounter, 61
A Matter of Trust, 151
A Pathway to Peace, 170
A Rainbow of Hope, 79
A Ray of Hope, 168
A Room of Her Own, 167
A Straighter Path, 110
Along Life's Way, 98
Along the Journey of Faith, 182
Altered Awareness, 50
An Unmovable Force, 165
Another Way, 81
Answering God's Call, 84
At Work, 134
Awestruck, 144
Be Still, 52
Calming Protection, 130
Can It Be?, 38
Change Me, 10
Children of God, 17
Choosing Words Wisely, 78
Come to Me, Child, 173
Cultivating Patience, 63
Defining Moments, 126
Don't Doubt God's Love, 15
Eager Expectation, 75
Emergence, 159
Empty Sorrow, 3
Facing Tomorrow, 119
Finding Our Way Back, 16
Firmly Focused, 62

Focus, 146
Forever Changed, 85
Founded Fears, 58
Fruitful, 86
Gentle Thoughts, 71
God Alone Saves, 70
God Bless You, 138
God in Whom We Trust, 132
God Is Still in Charge, 27
God Reaches Back, 40
God's Faithful Handiwork, 107
Healing Hands, 117
Heart, Mind and Soul, 18
Heart's Desire, 131
Heavy Fog, 54
Help at Hand, 122
Here I Am, 8
Hide and Seek, 112
His Guidance, 88
His Healing Rays, 171
Holy Happiness, 101
Hope Abounds, 95
How Blessed I Am, 154
Humbled by the Crown of Thorns, 34
I Choose to Believe, 21
I Thirst, 149
I Trust in You, 158
Imagine, 143
Imitating Faith in Action, 68
In Need of Humbling, 64
In the Midst of the Mess, 4

In the Morning Stillness, 66
In Times of Trouble, 180
Inner Calm, 128
It Is Time, 14
Jesus Knows, 109
Justified by His Grace, 136
Keep Believing in God, 32
Knowledge Born of Patience, 96
Laced with Excitement, 91
Lessons in Love, 29
Letting Go, 28
Life without Trust, 118
Look Fully at the Lord, 53
Love in Full Bloom, 174
Love Is Patient, 80
My Life Is Blessed, 172
Newfound Clarity, 30
No Need to Fear, 156
On the Battlefield, 133
Our Gracious God, 94
Our Refuge, 141
Our Very Best, 164
Overflowing Compassion, 74
Pause to Ponder, 114
Possessing Everything, 89
Precarious, 124
Predestined, 178
Protected, 162
Protective Power, 115
Providing an Anchor, 24
Put in Perspective, 82
Put to the Test, 90

Radiating God's Love, 108
Rejoice in the Lord, 83
Renewed Strength, 99
Rest, 92
Restored Confidence, 93
Return to God, 77
Rock Solid, 137
Save Me from Myself, 145
Saving What Was Lost, 36
Seek Actively, 42
Seeking His Guidance, 26
Seeking Justice, 33
Seeking the Kingdom, 13
Shadows, 148
Simple Trust, 147
Soaring to New Heights, 176
Source of Strength, 12
Stay Close, 127
Streams of Light, 160

The Answer, 87
The Best Way, 23
The Fine Line, 19
The Firm Foundation, 161
The Light in the Darkness, 116
The Lord Provides, 185
The Master Chef, 6
The One Who Trusts, 157
The Open Door, 43
The Path of Salvation, 55
The Plumb Line, 153
The Promise Fulfilled, 142
The Tree of Love, 177
The Voice of an Angel, 166
The Way, 22
The Winds of Change, 97
There Are Consequences, 152
Throughout History, 150

Trust Completely, 184
Trust in the Lord, 139
Unconditional Love, 41
Unexpected Moments, 140
Unharmed, 121
Unlimited Patience, 56
Urgency, 20
Valuable, 72
Valuable Lessons, 163
Wait for the Lord, 49
Waiting in Hope, 57
Waiting Patiently, 51
Wait Steadfastly, 100
What a Comfort Thou Art, 120
When Trouble Is Near, 123
You Alone, 76
Your Amazing Grace, 135
Your Graciousness, 60

INDEX OF BIBLICAL REFERENCES

Acts 1:4b-5–**61**
Acts 13: 32-35–**174**
Acts 14:23–**160**
Acts 17:27-28a–**40**
Amos 5:4, 6a, 14–**43**
I Chronicles 5:20–**137**
I Chronicles 16:10-12–**34**
I Chronicles 28:9-10–**18**
II Chronicles 7:14–**30**
II Chronicles 15:2–**12**
II Chronicles 30:18c-19a–**42**
Colossians 3:12–**58**
I Corinthians 1:9*–**170**
I Corinthians 10:13*–**116**
I Corinthians 13:4-7–**80**
II Corinthians 1:3-6–**74**
II Corinthians 5:18-21–**161**
II Corinthians 6:4-10–**89**
II Corinthians 9:15–**170**
Daniel 6:23–**121**
Deuteronomy 4:29–**4**
Ecclesiastes 7:8–**96**
Ephesians 4:2-3–**71**
Exodus 14:31–**139**
Galatians 5: 22–**86**
Habakkuk 2:3*–**53**
Habakkuk 3:16b-19–**83**
Hebrews 2:13–**135**
Hebrews 6:12–**68**
Hebrews 6: 13-15–**94**
Hebrews 9:27-28–**55**
Hebrews 11:6–**32**
Hosea 10:12–**14**
Hosea 12:6–**77**

Isaiah 8:17–**112**
Isaiah 12:2–**119**
Isaiah 25:9–**133**
Isaiah 26:3-4, 8–**126**
Isaiah 28:16–**157**
Isaiah 28:16b-17a–**153**
Isaiah 30:15b–**109**
Isaiah 30:18–**60**
Isaiah 40:31–**99**
Isaiah 43:10*–**152**
Isaiah 50:10b–**138**
Isaiah 55:6-7–**10**
Isaiah 64:4–**99**
Isaiah 65:1–**8**
James 5:7-8–**63**
James 5:11–**90**
Jeremiah 14:22*–**156**
Jeremiah 17:5-8–**156**
Jeremiah 29:11-13–**27**
Jeremiah 39: 18–**124**
Jeremiah 49:11–**162**
Job 6:11–**54**
Job 18:11-14–**118**
Job 42:3b–**54**
John 3:12, 14b–**178**
John 5:30–**22**
John 12:36–**168**
John 14:1-3–**167**
I John 4:7-8**–**15**
I John 4:9-12–**184**
Joshua 14: 8*–**184**
Joshua 21:5–**163**
Jude 1:21–**182**
I Kings 22:5–**6**

II Kings 18:5-7a–**164**
Lamentations 3:19-24–**101**
Lamentations 3:22-26–**41**
Luke 9:10–**28**
Luke 10:27–**16**
Luke 12:31–**13**
Luke 19:10–**36**
Malachi 3:1–**15**
Mark 5:34–**120**
Matthew 6:33–**13**
Matthew 7:7-8–**29**
Matthew 8: 23-27–**128**
Matthew 11:28-29–**92**
Micah 7:7–**97**
Nahum 1:7–**180**
Numbers 20:12–**152**
I Peter 2:6–**157**
I Peter 5:6-7, 10–**98**
II Peter 3:9–**64**
II Peter 3:15a–**100**
Philippians 3:20-21–**50**
Philippians 4:8-9–**93**
Proverbs 3:5-6–**110**
Proverbs 8:17–**23**
Proverbs 14:29; 15:18–**78**
Proverbs 16:20b–**132**
Proverbs 19:11–**81**
Proverbs 20:22*–**82**
Proverbs 22:6, 17-19–**144**
Proverbs 28:5–**19**
Proverbs 29:25–**122**
Psalm 4:4-5–**116**
Psalm 5:1-3–**66**
Psalm 9:7-10–**33**

---

*   Contemporary English Version (CEV); **Darby Translation (DARBY); all other Biblical References on this page are quoted from the New International Version (NIV)

Psalm 13:5–**145**
Psalm 14:2–**37**
Psalm 20:7–**151**
Psalm 21:6-7–**178**
Psalm 22:4-11, 26b–**123**
Psalm 23–**185**
Psalm 24:3-6–**24**
Psalm 25:1-2–**108**
Psalm 25: 4-5**–**88**
Psalm 25:21*–**133**
Psalm 26:1b–**108**
Psalm 27:4, 8–**38**
Psalm 27:13-14–**49**
Psalm 28:7–**108**
Psalm 31:6b–**134**
Psalm 31:14-16–**117**
Psalm 32:8-10–**147**
Psalm 33:20-22–**57**
Psalm 34:4–**26**
Psalm 34:8, 10b–**21**
Psalm 37:3-6–**131**
Psalm 37:7-9, 34a–**79**
Psalm 38:15*–**128**
Psalm 40: 1-3a–**70**

Psalm 40:3–**166**
Psalm 46:10–**52**
Psalm 51:10–**51**
Psalm 52:8–**143**
Psalm 55:23b–**158**
Psalm 56: 3-4, 10-11–**115**
Psalm 62:1*–**90**
Psalm 62:8–**141**
Psalm 63:1a–**3**
Psalm 70:4–**26**
Psalm 71:5*–**121**
Psalm 78:46-47–**150**
Psalm 84:12–**172**
Psalm 86:1-4–**140**
Psalm 91:1-2–**148**
Psalm 105:3-4–**26**
Psalm 112:1, 7-8–**130**
Psalm 115:9-13–**154**
Psalm 118:8-9, 14–**173**
Psalm 119:2, 10, 176b–**16**
Psalm 119:41-45–**176**
Psalm 125:1–**165**
Psalm 130:5-6–**72**
Psalm 143:8–**159**

Psalm 145:15-16–**87**
Psalm 146:3-9a–**127**
Revelations 2:3, 7–**177**
Revelations 3:10–**62**
Revelations 13:10b–**82**
Revelations 21:5-6–**149**
Romans 8:19–**75**
Romans 8:22-25*–**95**
Romans 8:25, 28–**84**
Romans 8:28–**15**
Romans 9:33*–**157**
Romans 10:11-12–**146**
Romans 12:12–**76**
Romans 15:13–**171**
II Samuel 7:28–**142**
I Thessalonians 1:1-4, 9-10*–**91**
II Thessalonians 3:3*–**107**
I Timothy 1:16–**56**
Titus 2: 11-14–**85**
Titus 3:3-8a–**136**
Zechariah 8:19b, 21b, 22a–**20**
Zephaniah 2:3–**17**
Zephaniah 3:12-13–**114**

---

*   Contemporary English Version (CEV); **Darby Translation (DARBY); all other Biblical References on this page are quoted from the New International Version (NIV)

LIST OF POEMS BY CHAPTER

CHAPTER 1: SEEK ACTIVELY

Empty Sorrow 3
In the Midst of the Mess 4
The Master Chef 6
Here I Am 8
Change Me 10
Source of Strength 12
Seeking the Kingdom 13
It Is Time 14
Don't Doubt God's Love 15
Finding Our Way Back 16
Children of God 17
Heart, Mind and Soul 18
The Fine Line 19
Urgency 20
I Choose to Believe 21
The Way 22
The Best Way 23
Providing an Anchor 24
Seeking His Guidance 26
God Is Still in Charge 27
Letting Go 28
Lessons in Love 29
Newfound Clarity 30
Keep Believing in God 32
Seeking Justice 33
Humbled by the Crown of Thorns 34
Saving What Was Lost 36
A Beacon of Hope 37
Can It Be? 38
God Reaches Back 40
Unconditional Love 41
Seek Actively 42
The Open Door 43

CHAPTER 2: WAIT STEADFASTLY

Wait for the Lord 49
Altered Awareness 50
Waiting Patiently 51
Be Still 52
Look Fully at the Lord 53
Heavy Fog 54
The Path of Salvation 55
Unlimited Patience 56
Waiting in Hope 57
Founded Fears 58
Your Graciousness 60
A Close Encounter 61
Firmly Focused 62
Cultivating Patience 63
In Need of Humbling 64
In the Morning Stillness 66
Imitating Faith in Action 68
God Alone Saves 70
Gentle Thoughts 71
Valuable 72
Overflowing Compassion 74
Eager Expectation 75
You Alone 76
Return to God 77

Choosing Words Wisely 78	Put to the Test 90
A Rainbow of Hope 79	Laced with Excitement 91
Love Is Patient 80	Rest 92
Another Way 81	Restored Confidence 93
Put in Perspective 82	Our Gracious God 94
Rejoice in the Lord 83	Hope Abounds 95
Answering God's Call 84	Knowledge Born of Patience 96
Forever Changed 85	The Winds of Change 97
Fruitful 86	Along Life's Way 98
The Answer 87	Renewed Strength 99
His Guidance 88	Wait Steadfastly 100
Possessing Everything 89	Holy Happiness 101

CHAPTER 3: TRUST COMPLETELY

God's Faithful Handiwork 107	God in Whom We Trust 132
Radiating God's Love 108	On the Battlefield 133
Jesus Knows 109	At Work 134
A Straighter Path 110	Your Amazing Grace 135
Hide and Seek 112	Justified by His Grace 136
Pause to Ponder 114	Rock Solid 137
Protective Power 115	God Bless You 138
The Light in the Darkness 116	Trust in the Lord 139
Healing Hands 117	Unexpected Moments 140
Life without Trust 118	Our Refuge 141
Facing Tomorrow 119	The Promise Fulfilled 142
What a Comfort Thou Art 120	Imagine 143
Unharmed 121	Awestruck 144
Help at Hand 122	Save Me from Myself 145
When Trouble Is Near 123	Focus 146
Precarious 124	Simple Trust 147
Defining Moments 126	Shadows 148
Stay Close 127	I Thirst 149
Inner Calm 128	Throughout History 150
Calming Protection 130	A Matter of Trust 151
Heart's Desire 131	There Are Consequences 152

The Plumb Line 153	*A Ray of Hope* 168
How Blessed I Am 154	*A Pathway to Peace* 170
No Need to Fear 156	*His Healing Rays* 171
The One Who Trusts 157	*My Life Is Blessed* 172
I Trust in You 158	*Come to Me, Child* 173
Emergence 159	*Love in Full Bloom* 174
Streams of Light 160	*Soaring to New Heights* 176
The Firm Foundation 161	*The Tree of Love* 177
Protected 162	*Predestined* 178
Valuable Lessons 163	*In Times of Trouble* 180
Our Very Best 164	*Along the Journey of Faith* 182
An Unmovable Force 165	*Trust Completely* 184
The Voice of an Angel 166	*The Lord Provides* 185
A Room of Her Own 167	

ABOUT THE AUTHORS

Poet Mary Morgan Brown, a reflective, powerful, penetrating, pensive writer and educator, shares her second book, *Seek, Wait, Trust: Poems for Navigating the Spiritual Journey* which includes prayers authored by her husband of eighteen years, the Reverend Dr. Greggory L. Brown. In addition to her first book, *Love is the Remedy: Poems for a Mending Heart*, the prolific author has a series of soon to be published children's books. Mary is a member of the *Society of Children's Book Writers & Illustrators* and is a certified *Amherst Writers* facilitator.

The Browns on a Spiritual Journey

A graduate of SUNY/Brockport & National Lewis University, Mary taught middle school for 30 years in Schaumburg, Illinois. She was an adjunct professor at DePaul University before moving to California to marry her beloved Gregg in 2004. With a heart to help heal the growing crisis of homelessness in the Bay Area, Mrs. Brown used her talents as a writer to work as Marketing Director at Christian Church Homes in Oakland until her retirement. The organization has a mission to provide affordable housing to low-income seniors.

Mary's professional honors include twice being featured in *Who's Who among America's Teachers*, receiving a nomination to the *National Association of Professional Women*, and being a finalist for a *Golden Apple Award*. Mrs. Brown has served on the Board of Lend-a-Hand Foundation, facilitating their Stay-in-School initiative, and she also mentors youth at Miracles of Faith Community Church, where her husband is Senior Pastor.

Gregg Brown's lifelong service to his Lord and Savior Jesus Christ includes charismatic preaching, powerful praying, holy boldness for racial equity and social justice, passion for feeding people in body and soul, a mission-driven ministry, as well as love and compassion for all. At Miracles of Faith

Community Church, ELCA, he has served a diverse urban neighborhood as a respected man of God, youth advocate, and community leader since 2003. His lifelong mission, built on the foundation of the demonstrative love of Jesus, has been to help the underserved with food, medical assistance, housing, and spiritual sustenance. His humble leadership and life-changing ministry have received local and national media attention, including *The New York Times*, *San Francisco Chronicle*, *East Bay Times*, *Chicago Tribune*, and *Amsterdam News*.

Dr. Brown received a B.A. degree in Mass Communications from Indiana University, a Master of Divinity degree from Union Theological Seminary in New York City, and a Doctor of Divinity from Pneuma Theological Seminary.

Before moving to Oakland, Gregg served as a minister at several churches in New York City and Chicago. Also an educator like his wife, he served as a professor at Jarvis Christian College in Hawkins, Texas. Additionally, his talents were displayed as the Executive Director for the Black Tennis & Sports Foundation; a Fundraising Consultant to the National Retired Basketball Players Association; and as president of the Northern California Interreligious Conference. In his early years of social activism, he chaired the Youth March for Jobs in Washington, D.C in 1978 to advocate for YEP (Young Employment Program), part of the Humphrey-Hawkins Legislation. Dr. Brown has been honored with the N.A.A.C.P. Merit Award, Man of the Year recognition from the American Biographical Institute, Outstanding Young Men of America Award, Civic Leader Award, Peacemaker Award, and Humanitarian of the Year Award.

The joint talents of First Lady Mary Brown and Rev. Dr. Gregg Brown of Miracles of Faith Community Church result in a reflective and robust reading experience in *Seek, Wait, Trust: Poems for Navigating the Spiritual Journey*. The Brown's interracial marriage has withstood the onslaught of hate and has equipped them to speak truth to power and give compassion to the powerless. Mary's reflective, piercing insight and Gregg's vigorous, Heaven-bound prayers will leave the reader revitalized and transformed for a closer walk with God and more loving interactions with people.

Made in the USA
Monee, IL
08 December 2022

20187063R10129